WHEN DARKNESS REIGNS

A TRUE STORY

PHILIP REMINGTON DUNN

www.servingcalifornia.org

Where Darkness Reigns/ Philip Remington Dunn.—1st ed.

Contact: Philip R. Dunn
PO Box 369
Malibu CA. 90265

Dedication

To Pastor Bob Herrera of
Victory Outreach of Ventura County
He showed me the way

Then Jesus said to the chief priests,
the officers of the temple guard, and
the elders, who had come for him,
"Am I leading a rebellion, that you
have come with swords and clubs?
Every day I was with you in the
temple courts, and you did not lay
a hand on me. But this is your hour
—when darkness reigns."
Luke 22:51

Contents

The Client

OF ALL THE prisoners I had ever visited, he looked the most out of place. Quiet and unassuming, he revealed none of the characteristics common to a convicted murderer.

The outward trappings were there: faded yellow jumpsuit over white T-shirt, white socks in open-toed flip-flop sandals, and, of course, the ever-present chains. Leg irons were shackled around each ankle and connected in a manner designed to punish the wearer for any stride beyond its limits, and belly chains were wrapped around his waist connected within a black plastic box from which cuffs emanated on either side, keeping his wrists locked below his stomach. But I had finally grown used to it; seeing past the stigma of his condition, I could detect none of the pathologies common to men incarcerated for so long. Not that he was unaffected, but instead the lack of expression on his face revealed a man who had long since killed off any overt signs of emotion.

Missing were the angry protestations about a conspiracy that had denied him his rights and convicted him without cause. Rather, he barely spoke at all, and when he did it was in hushed tones spoken so slowly that I wondered if he had trouble with the language. His Spanish surname supported this theory, but the absence of any accent revealed a deeper meaning. Each word was carefully chosen and reluctantly spoken as if he feared conversation. This further confused me until I remembered that he had recently been transferred out of Pelican Bay State Prison behind a gang-related homicide.

I should have anticipated the paranoia any prisoner would have talking to "the man." Though I never saw myself as the man, and it always offended me when someone else did, I could not deny that I looked like him. At six foot two inches tall, blonde hair and blue eyes, I had often been mistaken for a prosecutor. As a young public defender, I had so often been approached in court by police officers with subpoenas asking me, "Are you going to need me today?" that I had quit referring them to the district attorney. Instead I'd simply say, "I don't need you," and send them on their way. Perhaps this was beneath my dignity, or worse, but they always offended me to some degree, and I couldn't help but wonder about trained investigators who made such snap judgments.

So we were equally confused about one another. Our biases were born of experience, not prejudice. He hadn't seen as many bad lawyers as I had malevolent gang bangers, but the punishment he had endured during their watch more than tipped the scales in his favor. Even so, my cynicism was not easily shaken.

Having long since learned to rely upon instinct, I sensed nothing in his character consistent with his conviction. Even his background fought against the notion he was a killer. The shooting occurred just a month after his honorable discharge from a three-year stint in the army. Despite growing up in Oxnard's most troubled neighborhood, he had no record or known gang affiliation. No moniker, no tattoos, not even a graffiti citation—a remarkable achievement for a young man who had grown up without a father in La Colonia. It was as if he had started at the top: murder and attempted murder with the use of a firearm for the benefit of a criminal street gang. Most gangsters worked their way up to this pinnacle of gang banging with a series of lesser crimes, starting out as taggers, then graduating to assaults and perhaps some drugs along the way, their crimes growing more serious as each new conviction sent them on to gangster finishing school, juvenile hall, county jail and finally state prison. This guy's first arrest was the night of the shooting that had sent him away for life.

Still, it was his demeanor that surprised me the most. Short, perhaps five foot seven, and thin of build, light skinned as if he hadn't seen the sun in years (he hadn't), with short black hair and a pair of wire-rimmed glasses partially held together with tape that rested unevenly on his nose, he looked more like a computer nerd than a murderer. Even his speech didn't fit the profile—he never once cursed or spoke ill of anyone. Everything about him was inconsistent with his current predicament. Could this man actually be innocent?

I had always been a true believer, a compulsively competitive advocate relishing my role as the eternal underdog. My mother had raised me on scripture emphasizing care of the poor, the oppressed, the widowed and the orphaned as well as the need to visit those in prison. Consequently, public defending and then later private criminal defense came naturally to me. What is more, I cherished the freedom my profession provided. I was beholden to no one other than my client and my own personal convictions. What I loved, what I relished the most, what made all the pain and suffering I witnessed or even endured myself bearable were the victories. Each one was like the Miracle Mets winning the World Series, David defeating Goliath, one miserable client and his lawyer defeating the entire government, the law enforcement juggernaut, The People of the State of California.

What slowly drew me to Tony Estrada was the hope that he might be the one. I had come to see him looking for a reason to say no, my rational mind being aware of the personal cost involved and the power and commitment of the prosecutors who had already convicted him. But my heart spoke otherwise, in terms that could not be measured, in feelings so strong they could not be denied. By the end, I had agreed to take his case for nothing more than the honor of doing so and the prospect of some greater glory.

As I look back today, having lived the events I am about to relate, I am still convinced that had I read a work of fiction with the same story line, I would have dismissed the effort as a great tale having no connection with reality. What Tony Estrada endured at the hands of those charged with dispensing justice should never have happened, but it did happen, just as the pages that follow report it.

CHAPTER 1

The Homicide

FROM A BARRIO in Oxnard known as La Colonia, they venture out. They take with them a sense of hostility that only living on the wrong part of town can bring. Several of them claim to be "Colonia Chiques," a serious criminal street gang by any standard.

Tonight they are driving north, up the Southern California coast to Santa Barbara, to party at local clubs. Out on a Saturday night, all they want is a little dancing and a lot of drinking.

Their escape from the neighborhood starts a little after 10:00 p.m. on January 25, 1997. Before leaving, they stop for happy hour margaritas and then pick up some forties for the road trip ahead. Drinking games entertain along Highway 101, so that upon arrival everyone is well prepared to go clubbing.

Their final destination is the Hurricane Club, a small discotheque off of State Street, the most prestigious business address in the city. The usual Saturday night crowd fills the shops, bars and restaurants that define the tourist center of the city. They park in Municipal Lot 10, a multi-level parking structure behind the Hurricane. From Lot 10, they walk to the club together, entering through the front on State Street, passing the bouncers at the door without notice.

Inside, no one does much dancing, but they continue drinking throughout the night. As the evening wears on, their location shifts, from here to there, until they end up next to a group of young men from the east side of Santa Barbara.

"East Side" has already been identified by the Santa Barbara Police as a criminal street gang. In other jurisdictions like Los Angeles or even Ventura County, East Side may not have risen to such stature. They would not have been criminal—or violent—enough to rate the designation of a criminal street gang. But in Santa Barbara, enough crimes had occurred where someone had proudly claimed themselves to be East Side that law enforcement now tracked known associates of the gang.

The East Side homeboys party without dates, drinking and hanging around together. They keep to themselves, until Michael Chavez notices a particularly attractive young lady from La Colonia.

As the biggest and most aggressive member of East Side, Chavez believes he can make his move without fear of reprisal. Unfortunately, Carolyn Wright's boyfriend, Dino Ramirez, has other ideas about Carolyn's affections. With his not-quite-six-foot thin frame and impeccable grooming, Dino looks more like a lover than a fighter. Nothing about Dino's presence discourages Chavez. He considers Dino little more than a nuisance. With most of his homeboys from East Side present and accounted for, Chavez decides to make a move on the pretty "hyna"* from Colonia.

Dino won't let it ride as he calls upon his partner, Gilberto Zapata, to get his back. Though Gilberto is neither tall nor stout of build, he is the one always looking for a fight. Oblivious to the odds, Gilberto revels at the prospect of a challenge from another gang.

Various threats and taunts make conflict inevitable until Alfonso Rodriguez or "Capper" approaches East Side in an effort to make peace. The obvious leader of Colonia, Capper is their most powerful member. Well over six feet tall, barrel-chested and full of attitude,

---

* Hyna or *jaina* is a term commonly used by Hispanic men to refer to young (usually Hispanic) women. It is considered derogatory in some groups, while others use it as a term of endearment.

Capper's intervention draws everyone's attention. Dressed with purpose in jeans and an oversized untucked Pendleton shirt hanging below his hips, Capper projects the image of a serious gangster. He speaks softly for a big man, yet no one dares to talk over him. Capper commands the total respect of Colonia. Even the East Side homeboys sense he is the real deal. With but a few words, Capper calms both sides. Capper's words are delivered with respect, but his tone and demeanor insinuate violence. His subliminal message is clear: whatever East Side might be thinking, it wouldn't be worth it.

After Capper exerts his influence, things settle down, and it seems there was no disrespect intended, and no harm done. Unfortunately, Michael Chavez doesn't get it. He has the numbers and this is his 'hood. He can't resist pressing his advantage; once again, tempers flare. They stand chest-to-chest, bodies tense at the prospect of fighting, communicating in both heated words and contorted movements of the hand. Conflict of the most dangerous kind seems unavoidable. At this point, intervention from the bouncers is assured. As civilians just doing their job, their presence is tolerated. They take Colonia out the front door as the Chiques let East Side know they'd like to see them again sometime.

Out along State Street in front of the club, Colonia gathers at a large window looking back inside. Gilberto starts a heated argument with the bouncers at the door about the return of his five-dollar cover charge. Denied his cash, Gilberto goes to the window and frantically jumps up and down, inciting the East Side homeboys still inside. Arranging his fingers to form the letters "C" and "O" he further challenges East Side. Knowing the seriousness of the threat, the bouncers usher East Side out the back onto a poorly lit sidewalk next to Lot 10.

About fifteen East Side homeboys have now congregated on the sidewalk behind the club. They are hanging around trying to decide their next move, just as Dino and Carolyn walk by, heading for the parking lot. Seeing them, Michael Chavez goes straight for Carolyn Wright. Dino steps up, but Chavez pushes him aside with ease. Intimidated by the odds, Dino runs, heading down the lower parking ramp, leaving Carolyn alone with Chavez just inside the dimly lit structure.

Outside, La Colonia stragglers walk slowly to their cars before coming upon the rest of East Side still hanging out in back of the Hurricane. More gang signs are thrown, taunts repeated, and threats from both sides exchanged. Gilberto, never one to be outdone, runs to a bicycle leaning against a tree, picks it up and throws it high into the air at East Side.

Angered, East Side asserts their advantage by pushing Colonia further inside Lot 10 and then up against the interior walls. Seeing their peril, Dino returns to stand with his homeboys. Outnumbered nearly three to one, Colonia knows they are about to take a serious beating. The chant of "East Side" reverberates off the walls and beer bottles are heard shattering against the pavement as the circle surrounding Colonia continues to tighten.

Then, just as the homeboys from East Side begin to press their advantage, a man appears in the shadows of the stairwell, swiftly moving into the garage. As he comes up behind Colonia, the glint of a long-barreled, steel-plated, .38-caliber revolver can be seen in his hand. Muzzle flashes intermittently light up the darkened garage. Gunfire echoes off the walls as the shooter moves through the night, pulling the trigger.

In front for East Side, John Moreno falls first. A slug from the .38 strikes the middle of his neck, passing straight through. Moreno clutches the wound with both hands as he stops to consider the blood seeping through his fingers. He hesitates just a moment before losing consciousness and falling backwards to the pavement below.

The tide of battle has now shifted in favor of Colonia as cruel reality hits East Side with each new explosion. East Side turns to run in all directions, but the shooter pursues them with the enthusiasm of a hunter stalking big game. Moving forward with long, slow strides carefully designed to keep the sights of the revolver in line, he shifts from one target to the next. With each shot fired, the smoke of spent cartridges mixes with the flashes of new explosions as the shooter empties one chamber after another.

In the middle of the East Side pack, Mitchell Sanchez turns to run back from whence he came, but it's too late. A bullet slams into his head at the base of his skull, finally coming to rest in the center of his brain.

Sanchez falls face first to the pavement, where he remains, never again to move on his own.

Then, in a style uniquely their own, the Colonia Chiques move in on their fallen prey. Gilberto runs to the shooter and takes the gun from him in an exchange so smooth it looks rehearsed. Gilberto then runs back to where Moreno and Sanchez lie helplessly bleeding to death on the sidewalk.

As Gilberto reaches Moreno, he bends down, puts the barrel of the gun to the top of Moreno's forehead; and pulls the trigger. Gilberto tenses for the explosion, but nothing happens. All he hears is the sharp click of the firing pin striking an empty cartridge. Gilberto screams with rage as his lust for violence is frustrated again. He soon fulfills his passion, though, as he puts the gun in the palm of his right hand and uses it as a club to beat Moreno back and forth on both sides of his face. With each new blow, blood spatters into the air and onto the gun, leaving evidence in every crevice of the weapon.

Dino, having run to where Mitchell Sanchez lays, uses the heel of his boot to stomp Sanchez's face while taunting, "You're not so tough now, are you, motherfucker?" The other remaining Chiques break into a victory chant of "Colonia—Coloonia—Colooonia" that grows ever louder as they come together to encircle their fallen foes. It is the sound of sirens in the distance that finally signals the end of Colonia's game. They take off running in all directions in what looks like a designed play to avoid apprehension.

Patrons drawn by the sound of gunfire turn to see Colonia's escape. They witness three Hispanic males running down the sidewalk. They see a black, two-door sedan cross the street and pull up alongside them. Driven by a young woman with long dark hair, it hesitates just long enough for them to jump inside. Their timing is perfect. Just as they speed away, Officer Clouse comes racing down the street in an unmarked car. The onlookers gesture toward the fleeing black sedan, but Clouse is focused on points of egress and ingress. He stops in front of the parking lot exit to prevent other cars from leaving. The black sedan gets away cleanly.

Leaving his car, Clouse runs inside. He sprints to where Mitchell Sanchez and John Moreno are bleeding to death on the pavement. He sees what he believes to be brain matter on the cement next to Sanchez, and concludes that he is beyond hope. He then goes to Moreno just as the paramedics arrive. Moreno is bleeding from wounds in both the front and back of his neck. The smaller entry wound is only oozing red. It is the larger exit wound that is creating the growing bloody pool beneath his head. His condition is grave. Clouse calls the paramedics over, and they begin an effort to save his life.

As Clouse leaves Moreno and Sanchez to investigate the scene, his attention is drawn to a Hispanic male walking down the upper ramp. He notices the man is not watching the crime scene like other bystanders, but rather walking aimlessly down the pavement. Clouse approaches the man, ordering him to stop. His response is incoherent. Clouse notices that his right hand is in his back pocket. Fearing he might have a weapon, Clouse grabs him by the arm, twisting it behind his back and pushing him up against the back of a nearby car. Clouse then removes what is known as a leatherman's tool from the pocket. It is a multi-purpose tool, with many accessories, but now only the knife blade is extended.

Clouse questions the man about the shooting to no response. He then removes the handcuffs from his belt and slaps them on the man's wrists. His arrest complete, Clouse transports his suspect to jail. The man makes no further statements, but later in the night a police technician rubs cotton swabs on the back of both hands. Subsequent testing reveals particles consistent with gunshot residue on the back of his left hand, and particles unique to gunshot residue on the back of his right hand.[1]

On the way to the hospital, Mitchell Sanchez dies of a gunshot wound to the head, and he is pronounced dead on arrival. John Moreno hangs on to life until he reaches the hospital, where he undergoes emergency surgery. His condition remains critical for weeks. Ultimately, Moreno survives but never fully recovers.

Upon learning of the death of Mitchell Sanchez, homicide detectives go to the jail cell where the suspect, Tony Estrada, is being held. There, he is arrested for the murder of Mitchell Sanchez and the attempted murder of John Moreno with the use of a firearm in a gang-related homicide.

CHAPTER 2

The Prosecution

THE RESPONSIBILITY FOR prosecuting the Lot 10 homicide went to Santa Barbara District Attorney Thomas Sneddon. As a district attorney, Tom Sneddon was unusual in that he had not lost all familiarity with the courtroom. Most D.A.'s devote their time to administrative and political issues and assign all of their prosecutions to deputies. Tom Sneddon, however, was one of the few that would still try cases. Sneddon's "tough on crime" reputation was well established due to his aggressive style and relentless pursuit of the defendants.

Despite the high-profile nature of the Lot 10 murder, Sneddon assigned it to one of the most senior and trusted prosecutors, Hilary Dozer. Dozer was in his late forties and stood just under six feet tall with a slim build, closely trimmed moustache, and short brown hair just beginning to grey at the temples. His demeanor was stiff and military in style—the kind of man who would wear the American flag as a tie the day after the Fourth of July. He embodied a law enforcement prototype, invoking the image of "Dick Tracy," as one local newspaper would later comment.[2]

As a career prosecutor, Hilary had done it all. He had tried countless cases, establishing himself as a hard-nosed prosecutor. The hundreds of defendants he had convicted were serving thousands of years of time in prison. Within the criminal justice system, Dozer was known as a law enforcement hard-liner—courageous, reluctant to plea bargain, and willing to go to trial on a hard case. Dozer would rather spend his nights and weekends preparing for trial than make a deal for a defendant whom he believed was guilty. Not surprisingly, Dozer was a favorite of local law enforcement.

Hilary Dozer's detractors, however, described him as "arrogant and mean-spirited," with a tendency to grandstand.[3] These comments came following Dozer's one great defeat when he ventured into politics. In 1996, Dozer ran against a sitting judge for a position on the Santa Barbara Superior Court. Dozer openly attacked Judge James Slater as a liberal, sympathetic to criminal defendants. His public attacks were ultimately successful as Judge Slater dropped out of the election in September 1996. This opened up the race for other candidates. Finally, after a hard-fought campaign, Municipal Court Judge Frank Ochoa prevailed in the election. Dozer, denied the power of a judgeship, made a quick comeback as the prosecutor in charge of gang crimes.

Whenever a gang crime occurred, local detectives consulted Dozer. Such was the case with the Lot 10 homicide. Dozer immediately became involved in the investigation, since it was an invasion of the tourist section of the city by gangsters from another jurisdiction. It was the kind of high-publicity murder that Hilary Dozer loved to work.

The morning after the homicide, the City Police assigned a team of detectives to the case. The shocking nature of the murder and its proximity to downtown, with its potential impact on the tourist industry, created a great deal of pressure to resolve it quickly. All available resources were assigned to the matter.

Since they already had a suspect in custody, it was an easy matter to determine who the other suspects might be. Tony Estrada was from Oxnard, and Oxnard meant Colonia Chiques. A call was made to the Oxnard Police Department requesting assistance in the investigation. By then, Santa Barbara police had secured a videotape from the Hurricane showing Colonia entering the nightclub. Since they could see Estrada on the tape, all they had to do was find out who was with him. The man for the job was Oxnard gang expert Detective Dennis McMaster.

Detective McMaster stood six feet tall, strong and broad-shouldered, with piercing blue eyes and very little hair left on his head. McMaster had made a career of breaking up street gangs in Oxnard. He had grown up in the area and witnessed their destructive influence on the Oxnard community first-hand. While still in high school, McMaster signed up as an Explorer Scout with the Oxnard Police Department. Upon graduation, he attended the Police Academy, became a patrol officer and rose to the level of detective, first in narcotics, and then in gang crimes.

McMaster was the ultimate street cop. He was a one-man army, possessing a computer-like memory, making it possible for him to remember everyone he had ever encountered. McMaster was a law enforcement true believer. He became a cop in an effort to make the world a better place, and his way of doing it was putting all the bad guys away for as long as possible. McMaster was a "cop's cop," well respected and liked by everyone in law enforcement.

Needless to say, Dennis McMaster's aggressive style and total commitment to winning did not make him popular with local defense attorneys. From the moment he first hit the streets in Oxnard, McMaster was red-flagged by the defense. His countless arrests and questionable probable cause quickly caught the attention of the Ventura County Public Defender's Office.

Since public defenders handle about eighty percent of the criminal cases within their jurisdictions, they quickly become familiar with the police officers assigned to patrol. This is particularly true if the officer is as aggressive as McMaster. It was not long before McMaster was identified by the true believers on the defense side as a rogue cop who had no regard for people's constitutional rights, and particularly the rights of those who lived in La Colonia.

With his extraordinary memory and zest for the work, McMaster was able to interview virtually every gang member in Oxnard. He began keeping detailed computer records of names, dates of birth, nicknames, known associates, particular gang affiliation, tagging crews, relatives and prior criminal history.

Though Oxnard would always have several different street gangs at any one time, they were all eventually dominated by the Colonia

Chiques.* This made Colonia McMaster's personal project. Oxnard would be a better place if only he could break up the Colonia Chiques.

The first thing asked of McMaster was a review of the videotape of the entrance of the Hurricane on the night of the homicide.[4] McMaster easily identified Alfonso Rodriguez and his wife Monica, along with Gilberto Zapata, Dino Ramirez and Alfonso Martinez. McMaster was also able to provide their "monikers," or street names. Alfonso Rodriguez was known as "Capper," Gilberto Zapata "Zap," Dino Ramirez "Pretty Boy" and Alfonso Martinez "Little Capper." The only person that McMaster was unable to identify was Tony Estrada.

Gang monikers are not unlike nicknames young men have given their friends for centuries. Typically, they pertain to a particular look, experience or personality trait latched onto by their peers. So, for example, Dino Ramirez was "Pretty Boy" due to his propensity to flirt with the girls, and Gilberto Zapata was "Zap" not only because it was short for his last name, but also due to his quick temper that emerged like an electrical charge.

As a result of McMaster's identification, Dozer had arrest warrants issued for Capper, Zap, Pretty Boy and Little Capper. Search warrants were also produced for the residences and vehicles of the suspects.[5] Different teams of law enforcement from both Santa Barbara and Oxnard were assembled for the service of warrants.

In the evening hours of January 26, 1997, five different teams made the raids. Dino Ramirez, Alfonso Rodriguez and Alfonso Martinez were home when the warrants were served, so they were quickly arrested and taken to the Santa Barbara jail. Gilberto Zapata could not be found and became a fugitive with an arrest warrant for murder.

All of the searches netted some type of evidence that could be used against the suspects. For instance, clothing at the homes of Gilberto

---

* On March 23, 2004, the Colonia Chiques received national publicity after the Ventura County District Attorney's Office filed for a permanent injunction against the "criminal street gang." The subsequent injunction was the most pervasive and controlled the largest geographic area of any gang injunction ever issued, under the theory that street gangs are a public nuisance. The lead Deputy District Attorney on the injunction was Senior Deputy Bill Haney. (People v. Colonia Chiques, Ventura Superior Court Case No. CIV 226032.)

Zapata and Dino Ramirez was found to contain small blood stains. Gang material, including photographs of various members flashing gang signs, and different types of Colonia graffiti were found in all of the residences, but particularly in the home of Alfonso "Capper" Rodriguez.

Also taken in the searches were three cars believed to be involved in the crime. The first car impounded was a late model black Ford Mustang owned by Capper and his wife Monica. An inspection of the car revealed that it had recently been carefully cleaned. The second car was a black Honda Civic registered to Carolyn Wright, Dino's girlfriend. A search of this car revealed what appeared to be the traces of blood on the rear floorboard behind the driver's seat.

Despite the thoroughness of the searches, none of them produced a murder weapon. Rather, a revolver was found the next day on the second floor of Lot 10. The gun was in plain view in a parking stall near the stairwell going down to the front of the lot. It appeared that the gun had been left underneath a car sometime the night before, and then became visible when the car left the lot the next day. An inspection of the gun revealed that it had five spent .38 caliber cartridges in its chambers, with the sixth chamber being empty.

The next stage of the investigation was the interrogations of the suspects. It is well known within law enforcement circles that despite the requirement to give a "Miranda Warning" regarding their right to remain silent[6], criminal suspects usually talk about their arrests. The desire to talk can make it easy for an experienced detective to secure a waiver of the right to remain silent and start an interrogation. If the suspect is guilty, he will usually lie about the details of the crime, and those lies can then later be used against him. The false statements are then used in trial to "impeach the defendant" and reveal his "consciousness of guilt."[7]

After the advisement, Dino Ramirez waived his rights and started describing the events of the previous night. Dino told of the confrontation between the two groups in the Hurricane and how it spilled over into parking Lot 10. He went on to distance himself from the shooting by stating that he was running out of Lot 10 when he heard the gunshots. He said that he had not seen who did the shooting and was in no way responsible for what happened. When confronted with the fact that witnesses had seen him kicking Mitchell Sanchez as he lay bleeding on the sidewalk, Dino realized his mistake, finally saying, "I think I may need a lawyer." The interview was then terminated.

Alfonso Martinez's interview was less productive. He also waived his Miranda rights and adamantly maintained that he had remained inside the Hurricane with his girlfriend when the shooting occurred. Despite the detective's best efforts to poke holes in his statement, he never varied from his position that he knew nothing of the shooting and wasn't present when it occurred.

The most challenging of the interrogations was Capper's. Ultimately, Capper made a statement, but the circumstances are in dispute. The detectives simply noted that Capper waived his Miranda rights and then described how he had gone to Santa Barbara, with his wife doing the driving. Capper said that he and Monica had not parked in Lot 10, but rather down the street from the Hurricane off of State Street. Capper was present during the first confrontation between East Side and Colonia. His version was that it occurred over Tony Estrada's girlfriend, Veronica Mendez, and Estrada at one point pulled out a knife. That's when Capper said he stepped up and acted as peacemaker. He thought everything would be cool until the club's bouncers asked them to leave. After being escorted out the front, Capper and Monica walked down State Street away from Lot 10 and then drove home to Oxnard. Understandably, Capper was unable to identify the shooter or otherwise tell how it happened.

The unofficial version of Capper's statement is a little more revealing. He would later report that when first confronted by the detectives, he immediately invoked his Miranda rights and refused to talk. However, as he told it, the detectives then threatened to arrest Monica if he didn't talk. If Capper wanted to avoid his wife being arrested, leaving his two young sons without a mother or father, he had to make a statement. Capper felt he had no choice, so he waived his rights on the record. Remarkably, despite the fact that Monica fit the description of the driver of the getaway car, a black sedan she and Capper owned, she was never arrested or interrogated as a suspect.

After interviewing all of the Colonia suspects, the detectives' next course of action was to seek out and interview witnesses. All witnesses needed to be interviewed, but those who observed the shooting were critical. First up were all of the East Siders in Lot 10.

Standard procedure for a suspect identification involves the use of a photo identification "six pack," where a photograph of one of the suspects, usually a booking photo, is placed among five other photographs of individuals of the same approximate age, race and facial characteristics. The witness is then informed that the suspect's photo may or may not be one of the six before them. He is then asked if any one of the six is someone involved in the shooting. If the witness makes an identification, he is asked to initial below the photograph and describe the strength of his identification and what he remembers about the suspect. However, for reasons never explained, Santa Barbara law enforcement chose not to use standard procedure. They instead used the videotape of the entrance to the Hurricane. They played the videotape of Colonia entering the Hurricane and asked the East Siders if they could identify who was in Lot 10 at the time of the shooting.

Gilberto Zapata and Dino Ramirez were the first to be identified. They were picked out as the two who kicked and beat John Moreno and Mitchell Sanchez as they lay bleeding on the sidewalk. Identifying the others was more difficult. Neither Capper nor Alfonso Martinez was identified by anyone. Tony Estrada was identified as being present in Lot 10, but only after everyone else had left the scene.

None of the East Siders identified the shooter. They gave various descriptions, most of which were of a large, heavy-set man with dark features, but they were unable to be more specific. This came as no surprise, nor should it have, since it is common in gang versus gang crimes for participants on either side to refuse to identify the shooter. This code of silence is an important and integral part of gang culture. A "true gangster" takes care of his own business and doesn't cooperate with police. He will seek his own justice somewhere down the road.

There was likely another reason no one from East Side identified the shooter. Colonia's reputation for retaliatory violence was well known, even as far away as Santa Barbara. Colonia had just proven their reputation was well deserved. If an East Side member violated gangster ethics by helping the police against a homeboy from La Colonia, some would think it courageous and others foolhardy. It is one thing to put oneself at risk, and another thing to involve one's whole neighborhood. After all, the gang knows where you live, and your neighborhood is only a drive-by away.

Since the participants in Lot 10 wouldn't identify the shooter, detectives turned next to the civilian witnesses. The parking lot had many people moving in and out at the time, but no one could pick out the shooter. Then Charles Brodie emerged from the haze to offer the missing link.

Brodie had walked with his date into Lot 10 and was leaving in his car when the shooting occurred. He would later testify that he was heading down the exit ramp from the second floor when the traffic in front of him stopped. While adjusting his radio, he saw a man enter near the stairwell and move forward, shooting a gun. He described the gun as a semi-automatic. After the shooting, traffic in front of him broke up, and he left the parking lot. Frightened by the event, he drove north on Highway 101 to the city of Santa Maria, almost an hour away. It was there that he decided to call the police and tell them what he had seen.

Brodie spoke with a desk officer describing the event. He gave a sketchy description of the shooter, characterizing him as a fairly tall man with facial hair, perhaps a goatee. Finally, he reluctantly provided his address in spite of his concerns that he might have to testify in the future.[8]

An officer later interviewed Brodie at his home in another county. The officer came prepared to take a detailed statement, and he brought the videotapes taken in the Hurricane. The officer reported that Brodie remained reluctant to give the name of his date that night, allegedly because he knew it was a gang crime. Brodie provided few new details about the shooting until he saw the videotapes. Upon seeing the tapes of Colonia entering the Hurricane, Brodie got excited. "That's the guy," he exclaimed, pointing to Tony Estrada. "As far as I am concerned, that's the right guy."[9]

The case against Tony Estrada was now complete. He had been arrested at the scene of the crime. Gunshot residue had been found on the back of both of his hands, and an independent eyewitness had identified him as the shooter. The prosecution had all they needed to try Tony Estrada as the shooter in Lot 10.

CHAPTER 3

The Preliminary Hearing

ONCE A CRIME has already been investigated and the suspects have been arrested, the criminal system begins its process. The first court hearing is the arraignment, its purpose being the advisement of defendants as to the nature of the charges filed by the prosecution.[10]

In a practical sense, the most significant thing about an arraignment is the selection of a defense attorney. If the accused is wealthy enough, he can hire any attorney he chooses. However, in most criminal cases, particularly murder trials, defense attorneys are appointed by the court and paid for by the county. The first attorney to be appointed to an indigent defendant is usually a deputy in the public defender's office.[11] Since each defendant is entitled to his own attorney, and the public defender would have a conflict representing more than one defendant, individual private attorneys must be appointed to the remaining defendants. These lawyers are chosen from a panel of attorneys approved by the local judges. Being a panel attorney often accounts for most of the attorney's livelihood. So, panel attorneys have to be careful not to alienate the local bench, a potential conflict that does not go unnoticed by some of the system's more sophisticated defendants.

So when Tony Estrada, Alfonso Rodriguez, Dino Ramirez and Alfonso Martinez appeared at their arraignment, they were each assigned local panel attorneys to represent them. Tony Estrada was given to one of the local good old boys of the bar, Bill Duvall. Tall and unassuming, with light brown hair and eyes, Duvall was well liked by both the judges and prosecutors. Close to fifty at the time, Duvall was capable enough if sufficiently motivated. Though the preliminary hearing went on for weeks, nothing contained in the record indicates Duvall was an active participant. Perhaps he was saving his defense for the trial. The preliminary hearing began on February 19, 1997.

From the beginning, Hilary Dozer's presentation of the evidence focused on Tony Estrada. Testimony was presented about how he was captured at the scene of the crime and how gunshot residue was found on the back of his hands. This alone would have been sufficient to hold Estrada to answer the charges, but now they also had evidence of Tony's direct involvement. With Charles Brodie's identification of him as the shooter, Dozer would have little trouble convincing the judge that Estrada should stand trial on all of the charges.

The prosecution of the other defendants was not as easy. Michael Carty, the lawyer for Martinez, had carefully reviewed the Hurricane videotapes. Though it was often difficult to distinguish among individuals, it was still possible to identify Martinez, and since the tapes recorded the date and time, it was possible to establish that Martinez was still inside the club when the shooting occurred. Despite Dozer's best efforts, even he could not argue with the videotapes. At the conclusion of the hearing, Dozer dismissed the complaint against Martinez ("Little Capper"), and he was released from jail after serving some two and a half months in custody.[12]

As to the two remaining defendants, the evidence against Dino Ramirez was the strongest. Dino had clearly been identified in Lot 10 at the time of the shooting. Witnesses also identified him as the one who ran up to one of the shooting victims and kicked him while he lay bleeding on the sidewalk. The search of his home found clothing spotted with blood and a pair of boots that had been wiped clean, but still retained traces of blood on the heels. This evidence, along with

Dino's statement to the police, was more than enough to hold him to answer charges as an accomplice to murder.

The case against Alfonso Rodriguez was a different matter. Detective McMaster, testifying as a gang expert, was able to provide abundant evidence of Capper's involvement in the Colonia Chiques.[13] Capper had a significant criminal record, and he was well known for drug activity in Oxnard. Capper also had a reputation for violence. He had been a suspect in several shootings, but he had never been convicted. McMaster's opinion was his reputation for retaliatory violence was so powerful that no one would testify against him.

Obviously, Capper was a proud member of the Colonia Chiques, and he did not apologize for it. During the search of his house, the police found all kinds of evidence of gang involvement, including photographs of him and other members of Colonia flashing signs with one hand and carrying a gun in the other.

Capper did, however, have a couple of things going for him at the preliminary hearing. The first was his appointed attorney, James Crowder. Crowder was in his early fifties, which is the prime of a trial attorney's career. Crowder was of average height and build with a full head of neatly trimmed gray hair and a brush moustache that made him look professorial. When in court, Crowder was always impeccably dressed, and he moved about with the ease and grace of a man sure of his abilities.

At the preliminary hearing, Crowder was an active participant. He knew that there was little evidence linking his client to the shooting. No one would (or was willing to) testify that they had ever seen Capper in Lot 10. This was consistent with Capper's statement the night of his arrest. His defense was that he had tried to calm everyone down. In fact, one of the East Side gang members had even testified that inside the club he was a "cool peacemaker."[14]

When it came time for Crowder's closing argument, his remarks were not lengthy. He started off by thanking the court, and then a little diplomacy. "First, I would like to say I think this is a sad situation, where young people are going around killing each other." Moving along, he reiterated that Capper had been the "cool peacemaker," and there was no evidence contradicting his client's initial statement to the police.

Crowder did have one large hurdle to get over, which was all of the evidence supporting his client's reputation as a hardcore gang member. Crowder's argument was as simple as it was artful. He noted that everything tying Capper to Colonia was almost two years old. Crowder argued that his client had since married and had children and that people change, grow up, and grow away from their old ways. Since Capper hadn't been arrested within the last two years, he must have changed his lifestyle.[15]

Finally, it was Bill Duvall's turn to argue, and the transcripts are as follows:

<u>Court</u>: Mr. Duvall, let me hear an argument as to Mr. Estrada.

<u>Mr. Duvall</u>: Your Honor, I think that the prosecution's case has some glaring weaknesses, but as far as the preliminary hearing is concerned, we are going to submit it.[16]

While other lawyers made impassioned pleas for the release of their clients, Bill Duvall prepared a one-sentence concession speech. This was consistent with his effort throughout the hearing. Duvall was defending the "heavy" in the case—that is, the alleged shooter. His only defense was that someone other than his client was the one with such a malevolent heart that he ran into a crowd of young men and started shooting. Tony Estrada now knew that his appointed lawyer either didn't believe in his innocence or just didn't care. The impact of this revelation was hard for Estrada to fathom. "If my own lawyer doesn't believe in me, what chance do I have here?" The desperation felt only by those completely powerless in a world created by the powerful now descended upon Tony with devastating force. He was utterly helpless, caught in a system designed to crush those unable to defend themselves.

When Dozer finally argued, he spent much of his time trying to make a case against Capper on the theory that he was an accomplice to murder. He conceded he was unable to place him inside of Lot 10. The only pieces of evidence Dozer had that Capper was involved were statements by witnesses that the getaway car was similar to Capper's black Ford Mustang. They had testified that the driver looked much like

Capper's wife, Monica. Dozer argued that Monica Rodriguez rescued the fleeing Colonia Chiques from Lot 10, so Capper must have been in Lot 10 when it went down. As a hard-core gang member, his mere presence was enough to prove he encouraged the shooting.

Ultimately, the judge was persuaded by Crowder's argument. He remembered the testimony of Detective McMaster, saying that it made him look "for evidence about Mr. Rodriguez" and that the "Mr. Rodriguez we have here, there was another one referred to... was a real bad egg. He was involved in three assaults with a deadly weapon, lots of criminal activity, and so on. So, I had to look at that and say, but, well, that finally is not what we have here."

In conclusion, the judge stated that Capper's prior record caused "extra scrutiny," but he acknowledged that "people do change, and they grow older," which "may make a difference." Due to the lack of evidence against Capper, the charges against him were dismissed. Capper walked out of jail and returned home to Oxnard.[17]

Of the original five suspects in the Lot 10 homicide, only two were left. Gilberto Zapata was a fugitive with an arrest warrant for murder. Capper and Alfonso Martinez had been released from jail, with all charges against them dismissed. Only Dino Ramirez and Tony Estrada were left to take responsibility for the shooting of John Moreno and the death of Mitchell Sanchez.

CHAPTER 4

The Trial

ANGELA RODRIGUEZ, MOTHER of Tony Estrada, was more than disappointed with the defense given her son at the preliminary hearing. She made an appointment with Bill Duvall at the first opportunity.

Rather than defend himself, Duvall suggested she might want to hire private counsel and that it would probably be best to hire "a lawyer from another county." Angela sought no further explanation of Duvall, feeling she understood him perfectly. Angela went in search of private counsel.

Joe Lax was a well-known criminal defense attorney in Ventura County. At well over six feet tall, with a thin frame and long face, Lax's appearance in court evoked that of a Texas cowboy. His strong southern accent and easy-going style played well in old, rural Ventura County where, at about sixty years of age, he could still get away with wearing string ties and cowboy boots to court.

Lax had started his career as a deputy sheriff for Ventura County. After law school, he opened an office in Oxnard, where he had since been practicing criminal law for over thirty years. His slow style and soft manner of speaking were a source of frustration to judges and court reporters alike. Try as they might, no one could make Joe move any faster; the more they pushed, the slower and softer he spoke.

By the time Angela Rodriguez came to see Lax, he was winding down his law practice. Though he still had an office in Oxnard, his principal residence was in Las Vegas, Nevada. A high-stakes gambler, Lax now split his time between the poker tables of Las Vegas and the criminal courts of Ventura County.

Lax was familiar with both Colonia and their nemesis, Detective McMaster. Gang cases were a staple of his practice, and the parents of the accused were his best customers. He knew parents from Colonia often could not afford to pay what most attorneys wanted for a gang case, but Lax was different; he would take their case for what little they had. So when Angela Rodriguez offered him her life savings of $10,000 to represent her son in a murder trial, Lax took the money.

Lax may have been well known in Ventura, but that wasn't true for Santa Barbara. He had limited experience with Santa Barbara judges, and he had never met the likes of Hilary Dozer, an experience that he would never forget.

The case of the <u>People of the State of California v. Tony Estrada</u> had been assigned to Department One of the Santa Barbara Superior Court, Judge Frank Ochoa presiding. The significance of Judge Ochoa being assigned to the high profile Lot 10 murder could not have gone unnoticed in the district attorney's office. Less than two years earlier, Hilary Dozer had run against Frank Ochoa for the very judgeship that Judge Ochoa now held. Under the circumstances, Dozer could have disqualified Judge Ochoa, and no one would have thought the less of him.[18] But Dozer was not the kind of man who was concerned that a judge might be biased against him. Dozer's aggressive style had offended many judges in the past, so to him one judge was as good as the other.

The daunting task of reviewing all the discovery loomed as the first order of business for Lax. A legal term referring to all of the evidence and related information opposing sides in litigation must provide to one another, the discovery rules require the prosecution to provide their entire case to the defense. As a protection to the defendant, discovery has become a constitutional right. The landmark United States Supreme Court case of <u>Brady v. Maryland</u>[19] found that a criminal defendant has a due process right to not only the evidence against him, but also any evidence that might exonerate him. This places an ethical duty on the prosecution to give the defense evidence that may even hurt their case. The rule was created to protect against over-zealous prosecutors who might try to hide defense evidence to avoid an acquittal. In the high-stakes, overly competitive world of criminal jury trials, winning at all cost is not an uncommon attitude. Rules like the one made in <u>Brady</u> are designed to make sure that justice prevails over pride.

Though Lax had received a mountain of paperwork from Hilary Dozer, he also believed that there was information about the Colonia Chiques that he had not received. He had cross-examined Detective McMaster on more than one occasion, and he knew McMaster kept a large notebook on every suspect and every criminal incident attributed to the Colonia street gang. Since the complaint alleged the Lot 10 homicide was performed for the benefit of the Colonia Chiques, Detective McMaster's expert opinion would be needed to establish Colonia as a criminal street gang. McMaster would also have to testify about the level of commitment each Lot 10 participant had to Colonia, so Lax began making demands for police reports on the gang affiliation and criminal history of everyone in Lot 10 at the time of the shooting.

In response, Dozer said he did not have the requested discovery; if it existed at all, he said, it was at the Oxnard Police Department. When Lax went to Oxnard P.D., he was told nothing could be released directly to him; rather, it had to go through the Santa Barbara D.A.'s office. Judges are reluctant to get involved in discovery disputes, preferring to rely upon the attorneys to do the right thing. Since Lax never sought a formal order that could be enforced with sanctions against the prosecution, Judge Ochoa told the lawyers they should get together and resolve the issues among themselves. Joe Lax must have known that Alfonso "Capper" Rodriguez was a hardcore gang member with a long record of gang-related violence. His failure to force Hilary Dozer to provide this evidence might be hard to understand, but for a late night visit to his office by Capper himself.

Capper told Lax he was there to find out how the defense of his cousin Tony Estrada was coming along. Capper asked pointed questions about Lax's strategy and what evidence he intended to present. Lax, on the other hand, wanted to know what, if anything, Capper knew about the shooting. Both men traded off questioning one another, but neither was satisfied with the answers they were getting. Lax could not discuss the defense of his client with a former co-defendant. Capper said he knew nothing about the shooting since he was on his way home to Oxnard when it occurred. It wasn't long before Capper started getting hostile. Lax ultimately got up the courage to tell Capper it was time for him to leave. In a rare moment of self-control, Capper left without further confrontation. Lax, however, did not forget the incident and how incredibly menacing Capper could be in the moment.

The Lot 10 case was set for trial on October 14, 1997. Before the trial took place, however, something inexplicable occurred. Dino Ramirez appeared in court with his attorney and entered a plea of guilty to a violation of <u>Penal Code</u> §32 as an accessory after the fact.

A separate crime not related to the homicide, but only for conduct occurring after the shooting, the maximum possible sentence was thirty-six months in prison. It was a far cry from the twenty-five years to life that a conviction for being an accomplice to first-degree murder would have carried.[20] Hilary Dozer had made Dino Ramirez an incredibly sweet deal, considering all of the evidence of Dino's involvement in the homicide.

Eventually, the deal got even sweeter. When Dino entered his plea of guilty to the new charge, he was released from jail, and his sentencing was continued to a date after the trial. When sentenced, he was to be placed on probation with no additional time. While Tony sat in jail, Dino was set free with the understanding that he would never serve another day.

Even more startling, Dino's plea bargain provided that he would not be required to testify at the trial of Tony Estrada. Since he wouldn't be sentenced until after the trial, he still retained his Fifth Amendment right to remain silent.[21] Ordinarily, such a generous deal would require the recipient to testify against the remaining defendant. In a difficult prosecution, such an agreement would be needed to solidify the People's case. The strength of the testimony and the substantial risk taken by the defendant, now turned informant, would be justification for the light sentence. However, nothing more was required of Dino. He simply came to court, entered his plea of guilty to being an accessory after the fact, and went home to Oxnard. This left only Tony Estrada to stand trial for the Lot 10 shooting.

Dino's release was devastating to Tony. Dino had been his cellmate and his only friend in jail. Before Capper's release, Tony and Capper had shared a cell. Though they had grown up together, their relationship was strained. On the outside, Tony enjoyed a certain amount of respect just being related to Capper, but on the inside Tony was the only one Capper had to bully. Capper continued as enforcer of the Colonia code of ethics. Everyone was suspected of being a snitch, even his cousin. When Capper was released, Tony was relieved to find out Dino would be his new cellmate.

With Dino gone, Tony was moved to isolation. For his own protection, he could not be released into the main population, because his crime accused him of shooting rival Santa Barbara gang members. In isolation, Tony spent twenty-three of every twenty-four hours alone in his cell. Every minute of every agonizing day served as a reminder of how completely he had lost control of his life. Within the barren confines of his existence, Tony started losing hope. He turned in on himself, his depression slowly becoming desperation, and then finally delusion. He lived out his life in a semi-conscious haze, which was only occasionally interrupted by the deputy assigned to guard him during his one hour of recreation a day. Tony knew the guard only as Mike. A very stern-looking man, tall, with broad, muscular arms and shoulders, Mike was obviously not a deputy to be messed with. Though respected by other deputies, Mike had no sergeant's stripes on his sleeves, but only three stars on his cuffs indicating over fifteen years of service. Most senior deputies avoided the harsh duty of the jail, having paid their dues guarding prisoners when they were young. Mike should have been a watch commander or detective by now, but instead he was working an indeterminate sentence in the jail. In spite of this, Mike never expressed a bitter word. Rather, he treated everyone, whether colleague or criminal, with respect.

Despite Tony's quiet ways, Mike made an effort to speak with him whenever he came on shift. It didn't take long for Mike to realize the state of Tony's mind. Instead of spewing anger like other isolation inmates, Tony had taken on the listless countenance of the severely depressed. Slowly, Mike began sharing his faith with Tony, and eventually, he even presented him with a Bible.

Steadily, Tony's spirits started to revive. Every day he devoured new pages of scripture, reading and then re-reading until he had committed large portions of scripture to memory. When confused or misled, Mike would gently check his progress, sometimes offering a different interpretation, and, more importantly, encouragement when needed.

Tony's new faith gave him the strength to endure his captivity. As the date of his trial drew near, Tony's courage grew—so much so that when offered a plea bargain of fifteen years to life, he rejected it out of hand. Tony had decided to risk it all (that is, the rest of his life) rather than take a deal that might have made him eligible for parole in about twelve years.

The trial finally got under way on October 14, 1997. After opening statements, the prosecution called its first witness, Officer Patrick Clouse. Following Clouse, Dozer presented his case mostly in chronological order. He would spend more than a month calling over sixty witnesses to the stand.

Perhaps the most significant was the expert on gunshot residue, an employee of the Los Angeles County Coroner's office who explained the significance of the residue found at the scene of the crime. Once this expert established the presence of gunshot residue on the backs of both of Estrada's hands, he explained how microscopic particles were taken from both hands the night of the shooting—that on the right hand there were unique particles of gunshot residue, and on the left hand there were particles consistent with gunshot residue. Unique particles are present only after a gun has been fired, whereas consistent particles may be attributable to something other than gunpowder. The expert's direct testimony then concluded with the opinion Tony Estrada had either personally discharged a firearm or otherwise had his hands in an environment where gunshot residue was present.

On cross-examination, Lax pointed out being in the presence of gunshot residue could include transferring it from either a gun after it had been fired, touching the hands of an individual who had recently fired a gun or standing near a gun when it was fired. In that regard, the gunshot residue expert gave his opinion that the environment in which a person might pick up residue would be approximately two and a half feet out from the side of the gun being shot, and as much as five feet in a spreading pattern coming out of the muzzle of the gun.[22]

In sharp contrast to this scientific opinion was the subjective analysis presented to the jury by Detective McMaster. McMaster was called to testify as a gang expert regarding the Colonia Chiques of Oxnard. McMaster's credentials did not include a college degree in a field such as sociology or even criminal justice. Rather, his expertise was based upon personal experience and specialized law enforcement training.

McMaster had little difficulty establishing himself as a gang expert. Despite a steady stream of objections by Lax, Judge Ochoa allowed him to express all of his opinions.[23] McMaster began his testimony by defining a criminal street gang as "a group of people with an identifiable name who claim a particular geographical area and regularly participate in criminal activity." Armed with this broad definition, McMaster then easily concluded Colonia was such a criminal street gang. He did this by first providing a little history about the City of Oxnard and its primary barrio, La Colonia.

Oxnard had always been dependent on two sources of employment for its citizens: Point Mugu Naval Air Base and the rich surrounding farmland best known for its strawberry fields. With the prevailing influence of the Pacific Ocean, Oxnard's climate is one of the most temperate in the world. Rarely does the thermometer dip below fifty, or much above eighty degrees, making it possible for expert growers to get as many as four pickings a year. Thus, there has always been a great need for laborers to work the fields. Like many farm towns in California, Oxnard has always been a divided city. On one side of the railroad tracks is the town center, with its aging brick buildings and modest but well-maintained homes; on the other side are decaying apartment buildings and small stucco houses with bars on the windows. The area known as La Colonia is where most of the farm workers lived.

Over time, most of the communities surrounding Oxnard grew in size and stature, like others in Southern California. Oxnard always lagged behind its neighbors in both prestige and wealth; its dependence on farming held it back from starting up new industries. Eventually, it gained a reputation as the highest crime area in Ventura County. It was in this environment that the Colonia Chiques formed.

In McMaster's opinion, the Colonia Chiques had been around for about twenty-five years. Original members were associated with various car clubs within the Oxnard area. Over time, disputes arose between members of the different clubs, which sometimes ended violently. Thereafter, the clubs were influenced by parolees who had received an education on gangsterism in prison. In the early days, prisoners out of Ventura County did not go in as gang members. Upon release, however, they were well versed in the prison gang lifestyle. The gang subculture was then taught to other young men on the streets of Oxnard. Out of this, the Colonia Chiques were formed: "Colonia" for the area where they were from, and "Chiques" meaning boys in Spanish: Colonia Boys, or as they would have it, Colonia Homeboys. As time went on, Colonia grew in numbers. At the time of Detective McMaster's testimony, he had documented over 1,200 members. Membership had expanded beyond the Colonia and into almost every other part of Oxnard. As the gang grew, so did the number of crimes it committed. McMaster alone had investigated over two hundred fifty gang-related acts of violence associated with Colonia.

McMaster explained that gang behavior was not just related to criminal acts, but also to various signs and rituals. For instance, the "tagging" of various locations with Colonia graffiti was the way the gang marked its territory. Tagging let any young man within these boundaries know that he was on Colonia's turf. When they spotted an invader, Colonia homeboys would quickly surround the stranger and ask, "Where ya from?" There was no right answer to the question. If he were from La Colonia, and he was not a member, he had better be ready to join up. Living outside Colonia and being on their turf constituted a serious act of disrespect requiring a violent response. These are the rules of engagement that constitute the recruiting process of virtually all criminal street gangs. As long as the rules are enforced, new members are never hard to come by.*

---

* Author's note: When I first started representing gang members and learned of their recruiting methods, I was struck by how closely they resembled those used

After testifying about the history of gangs in general, and Colonia in particular, McMaster turned to the Colonia members involved in the Lot 10 homicide. When provided with the photographs seized in the search warrants, McMaster was able to identify everyone as an associate of Colonia. He pointed out how they proudly displayed gang graffiti in their homes and how they took pictures of one another using their hands to depict the letters "C" and "O," the gang sign for Colonia.

Though it would have been easy to describe all gang members the same, McMaster showed some fairness to individuals by developing three categories of membership. They were described as "hardcore," "associates" and "wannabes." These categories were then applied to the Lot 10 participants. Alfonso "Capper" Rodriguez was hardcore. Dino "Pretty Boy" Ramirez and Gilberto "Zap" Zapata were associates of Colonia. Tony Estrada, however, was not so easily categorized. Though he was in a few of the photographs with other gang members, McMaster knew of no prior police contact with Tony. His testimony concluded Tony appeared to be "associating with gang members."

Dozer then provided McMaster with all of the facts of the Lot 10 shooting and asked McMaster if he had an opinion whether or not it was committed on behalf of a criminal street gang. Not surprisingly, McMaster concluded that yes, this was a crime committed for the benefit of the Colonia Chiques. McMaster's testimony provided the jury with an expert opinion that addressed substantial portions of the charges against Tony Estrada—specifically, that the homicide was done at the direction of the Colonia Chiques street gang and that Estrada must have been associated with the gang when it occurred.

As always, McMaster's testimony devastated the defense. Since McMaster was the only known expert on Colonia, Lax was unable

---

by Adolf Hitler's Brown Shirts in post-World War I Germany. Not only did these early Nazis bully young men into joining them by beating up anyone in a beer hall not wearing a "brown shirt," but Hitler also designed symbols and rituals that clearly labeled his supporters as separated from and hostile to everyone else. The most obvious of these symbols was the Nazi flag with the Swastika designed by Hitler himself, right down to the selection of the "colors" (red, white and black). Source: Rise and Fall of the Third Reich by William Shirer, Chapter 1, Birth of the Third Reich, the Beginning of Nazi Germany.

to offer a contrary opinion. He was reduced to cross-examining McMaster on his favorite subject. McMaster had no difficulty on cross-examination, and so his opinion went to the jury largely unchallenged.[24]

Perhaps the best moment in the prosecution's case came when they called Charles Brodie. Brodie, in contrast to the other eyewitnesses, came in and boldly identified Tony as the shooter. When confronted on cross-examination that he had initially described the shooter as being taller and heavier than Tony, Brodie either did not recall or did not agree with the earlier statement. Brodie was now very sure of what he remembered, and he would not be shaken from it. The more Lax pressed him on his earlier statements, the more adamantly he denied them.[25]

Finally, on November 17, 1997, Hilary Dozer called his last witness, and the People rested. Lax now presented the defense case. In stark contrast to the prosecution, Lax called but five witnesses, only two of whom were of significance.

Lax called a forensic psychologist specializing in eyewitness identification. Dr. Shomer's credentials were impeccable. He had received both his bachelor's and doctoral degrees in psychology at UCLA. He then accepted a faculty position at Harvard, followed by a tenured position at Claremont College. For twenty years, he had been researching perception and identification of eyewitnesses in criminal trials.

Dr. Shomer's testimony considered the circumstances under which Brodie identified Estrada as the shooter. Brodie witnessed the shooting under life-threatening circumstances at a substantial distance. Brodie's identification of Estrada using the Hurricane videotapes violated standard line-up procedures. Typically, a witness is provided photographs of individuals with similar hair color, facial features and race. In the Estrada case, no such impartial procedure was used.[26] To Dr. Shomer, the flaw in using the videotape was its inability to exclude a suspect. Anyone identified would have been present at the scene of the crime.

After Dr. Shomer, Lax called Carolyn Wright, Dino's girlfriend. Her testimony provided a few details about what happened both before and after the shooting, but since she was hiding outside Lot 10 when the shots were fired, she did little to help Tony.[27]

The last witness called by Lax was Tony Estrada. Tony had no idea Lax wanted him to testify. He hadn't talked with his attorney in weeks, and there had never been any discussion about testifying. Tony quickly gathered his courage, however, and went to the witness stand intent on telling his story. Lax started with how he had been released from the army and then lived in Oxnard for only six weeks before the shooting. Since Tony's commitment to the army had been three years, he obviously was not an active member of the Colonia Chiques. This was a good fact for the defense.

Lax should have stopped there, but he could not resist having his client review all of the gang materials recovered by the warrants. He made Tony explain Colonia Chiques' gang signs, clothing and graffiti. Having grown up in Oxnard, Tony couldn't deny that he was familiar with the gang—everyone who lived in Oxnard was. Unfortunately, with each explanation Lax demonstrated closeness between his client and the gang.

Eventually, it was Tony's own words that hurt him most. He told the jury that he was drunk when he left the Hurricane, but he remembered he was walking with his girlfriend, Veronica Mendez, when he first noticed there was trouble brewing. Right after entering Lot 10, someone came up on his right, firing a gun. He put his hands up over his face, ducked down and screamed "NO!"[28] Even so, he was able to observe Mitchell Sanchez and John Moreno being hit by bullets. He ran to the stairwell and went up to the second floor. His car and girlfriend were nowhere to be found, so he walked down the upper-level ramp toward the first floor until he was confronted by Officer Clouse and arrested.

As is the case with most defendants, the problem with Tony's testimony was not what he remembered, but what he didn't remember. The only person Tony testified he saw in the parking lot was his girlfriend, Veronica Mendez. When asked about anyone else, he said he couldn't be sure or he didn't remember. He didn't remember if anyone ran up to Moreno or Sanchez after the shooting. He did not recall anyone kicking or beating them with a gun. The only thing Tony was sure of was that he was not the shooter. Whether one of his friends did the shooting or beat the victims afterward was something he knew nothing about. On this note, Lax concluded his client's testimony.

Hilary Dozer could not have been happier; he lived for moments like this. Lax had let his client testify, and Dozer was sure he had lied. Pointing out the half-truths and inconsistencies of Estrada's testimony would be Dozer's finest moment in the trial.

As he began his cross-examination, Dozer knew that he had to lock Tony into a set of facts from which he could not later escape. The testimony proceeded as follows:

<u>Dozer</u>: [Regarding street gangs] There is a code of silence isn't there?

<u>Estrada</u>: Code, what do you mean? I don't understand.

<u>Dozer</u>: In other words, one gang member doesn't testify against or talk about or finger another gang member, isn't that true?

<u>Estrada</u>: That's not true.

[Objection by Lax, overruled by Court]

<u>Dozer</u>: So, you are not aware of that being a problem at all?

<u>Estrada</u>: That's not true at all. I wouldn't want to ... if I knew something, I would tell you guys. I don't want to go down for something I didn't do.[29]

Tony couldn't admit to a code of silence for fear of further connecting himself to Colonia. Instead, he denied the code, thus destroying the only explanation for why he wouldn't implicate anyone else. Tony's denial of the code made it possible for Dozer to painstakingly review the established facts and then ask him why his testimony differed from everyone else's. Tony testified that five shots were fired by someone just to the right of him, but he didn't know who fired the gun. He never saw the gun given to anyone else, and he didn't know if Dino or Gilberto were ever in Lot 10. By the time Dozer concluded his cross-examination, Tony had denied the specifics of what happened so many times that the jury might wonder if he was even there—except for the gunshot residue all over his hands. Since he had to have been present at the time of the shooting, there existed only one reasonable conclusion about his testimony: he had lied about key details.

To conclude, Dozer set up one final question. Having a flair for the dramatic, Dozer couldn't resist taking the murder weapon in both hands, holding it up in front of Tony and demanding:

"Isn't it true, Mr. Estrada, that you took this gun, put it in your hands, leveled the sight, and just as you've been trained in the Army, fired off five shots directly at the people in front of you, just as you intended?"

Tony shot back:

"No, that's not correct."[30]

Still, the impact of the question made its mark on the jury. Dozer had shown them how the gun must have been fired and that Estrada knew how to use it.

Lax was then given a chance to rehabilitate his client, but the damage was done. The more Lax asked questions, the worse Tony looked. After letting Dozer take one last shot at him, the Court finally allowed Tony to step down and return to the safety of counsel table. Lax then announced that the defense rested. Thereafter, Dozer put on a short rebuttal, which offered little of consequence.

Next came closing arguments. Dozer's presentation was typical of most prosecutors. Since they present most of the evidence, prosecutors inevitably feel they must review it all and then argue how it applies to the law. This approach has the advantage of never overlooking a detail, but the disadvantage of losing one's most important points in an endless stream of complex law and facts. Dozer's closing didn't miss a single fact that might cast guilt upon Tony. His style was consistent and powerful, the strength of his personality taking complete control of the courtroom. When he finally concluded, everyone present was exhausted by the effort.[31]

Joe Lax's closing was similar in structure to Dozer's, a complete review of the evidence and all the relevant instructions on the law. His approach combined with his slow style and soft voice made it difficult for jurors to stay with him. In conclusion, Lax offered no impassioned plea demanding a finding of innocence. Instead, he just abruptly ended. His work done, he sat down next to his client, waiting to hear Dozer one last time.[32]

Dozer had now whipped himself into a frenzy. In fact, toward the end of Lax's argument, Dozer threw a pencil onto the counsel table so hard it bounced high into the air and landed on the carpet in front of the judge's bench. This hardly went unnoticed by the jury. Any other attorney might have objected, but Lax made no response.

Returning to the podium, Dozer no longer sought to indoctrinate his jurors. There was little he needed to respond to in Lax's closing. His rebuttal was brief and focused on a well-rehearsed conclusion.

Dozer told the story of the "Red Herring," a traditional tale prosecutors have told for almost as long as juries have been impaneled in criminal trials. Dozer told them its origin came from England a couple hundred years ago when the gentry were fox hunting. They would take a caged fox out to a field and release it. After giving the fox a sporting head start, they let their hunting dogs loose, and then the gentlemen on horseback went galloping after them. As time went on, a group of people emerged who were opposed to fox hunting. They considered it horribly abusive and demanded an end to it. In frustration, they devised a strategy. They would go to the fish market early in the morning and get the smelliest fish they could find, usually herring. Old herring took on a red hue. Then, they would place the herring in burlap bags and tie ropes round the tops. Before the fox hunt, they would throw the burlap bags all around. When the hunters released the dogs, they would go in search of the herring instead of the fox. Dozer then made his final point:

> "In this case, I think the defense counsel has essentially done the same thing. He has given you a matrix that has information that really isn't evidence in this case, and just like the person who throws those red herring off the back of

his horse, and goes back and forth through the field to get the dogs off track, the defense counsel has put issues out hoping that you will be side tracked.

I hope you stay in focus. I urge you to review your notes and ask for any re-read that you need, because the nature of the red herring is such that if you get side tracked, the only person that gets to run free is the fox. The fox is sitting over there, Tony Estrada. Thank you."[33]

At the time, Dozer didn't know just how profound his remarks would later become. His analogy could not have been better; Tony was like a fox. To the aristocratic English gentlemen and their hunting dogs that pursued him, the fox was a wild animal, clever enough to make the hunt a challenge. But for a few dedicated crusaders, the fox was an innocent creature to be protected from those who would take his life for the sport of it. Without the help of the crusaders, the fox would surely perish. With it, the fox had a sporting chance.

JURY DELIBERATIONS

On Friday, November 21, 1997, at approximately 3:30 p.m., Judge Ochoa gave the jury concluding instructions, and they went to the jury room to deliberate. Shortly thereafter, they went home for the weekend, only to begin their deliberations anew the morning of Monday, November 24, 1997. In a serious and complex case such as this, it would not be uncommon for the jury to stay out several days. This jury, however, was operating under a significant time constraint. Thursday, November 27, 1997 was Thanksgiving. All of the jurors had plans for the weekend; one even had a pre-paid vacation out of state. As deliberations dragged on, the pressure to come to a verdict grew intensely.

Finally, on the afternoon of Wednesday, November 26, 1997, the jury sent out a note saying they had reached a verdict as to one count, but were unable to reach a verdict as to two other counts. The judge asked the foreman whether it was his "considered judgment that the jury [was] hopelessly deadlocked and would be unable to reach a verdict even if given the opportunity for further deliberations."

The foreman responded, "I think that's true, yes."[34]

The breakdown in voting was 10–2, but it was not revealed which way the vote was going. A difficult discussion ensued between jurors and the judge about whether or not they should come back after Thanksgiving and continue deliberating. One juror was leaving for Hawaii the next day. However, he told the judge he had discussed it with his wife, and he was willing to stay on if the judge felt they could reach a verdict. Judge Ochoa then polled everyone, asking them if they believed further deliberations would be fruitful. One after the other said that they were hopelessly deadlocked. Only the foreman showed some hesitancy about declaring a mistrial and concluding the matter without resolution.

Judge Ochoa met in chambers with Lax and Dozer about what should be done. Lax felt there was no point in going any further, but Dozer vigorously disagreed. Ultimately, Judge Ochoa decided that they needed to come back. The jury went home for the Thanksgiving holiday.

On Monday, December 1, 1997, the jury returned to Judge Ochoa's courtroom at 9:00 a.m. They deliberated through the morning and into the afternoon without disruption. Then at 2:00 p.m., the foreman notified the bailiff they had a verdict. All interested parties were now summoned to Department One to hear the verdict.

The courtroom filled up quickly as family and friends of Tony Estrada, John Moreno and Mitchell Sanchez took up seats behind their respective advocates. The press was also present in large numbers, as the early afternoon verdict would come in just under newspaper deadlines. Tension mounted as everyone waited for the participants to arrive. The parties were just getting seated when the bailiff demanded "all rise" and Judge Ochoa took the bench. Fear now replaced tension as the bailiff brought the jury in, taking their seats for the last time. Judge Ochoa addressed the foreman, asking if they had a verdict, to which the foreman responded, "Yes." Additional sheriff's deputies now moved into position to quell any disturbance that might arise with the reading of the verdict. Starting with the first count, the crime of murder in the first degree, the jury found the defendant, Tony Estrada, not guilty.

Cheers and shrieks of joy from the family and friends of Tony Estrada filled the courtroom. But more experienced court watchers held their breath, knowing the jury may well have found Estrada had not committed first-degree murder, but he might still be found guilty of second-degree murder. Never hesitating, the foreman continued reading in a steady voice as Estrada's supporters quieted themselves to hear: "As to the second count, murder in the second degree, we the jury, in the above-entitled matter, find the defendant, Tony Estrada—guilty." The foreman then went on to further find Estrada had personally used a firearm in the commission of the crime and that the crime was committed for the benefit of a criminal street gang.[35] When at long last the reading of the verdict was finished, only the sobs of Angela Rodriguez could be heard coming from behind her beloved Tony.

The only business remaining was for the judge to order a sentencing date. The sentence, however, remained a foregone conclusion. Estrada was now a convicted murderer, and thus would almost certainly spend the rest of his life in prison.

The sentencing was to be heard on January 6, 1998. Just prior to the hearing, Joe Lax filed a motion for a new trial, alleging new evidence of his client's innocence. Unfortunately for Estrada, motions for new trials in criminal cases are routinely denied, and this is just what Judge Ochoa did. In doing so, he gave his opinion on Tony's guilt and the legitimacy of the jury's verdict. He placed the blame for Estrada's conviction squarely on the defendant himself.

"It is clear to the court that what happened is that when the defendant himself testified, there was at least one glaring inconsistency in his testimony.

He indicated that at the time the shooting occurred next to him, he ducked to the left and covered and then ran, and yet also described in detail the shooting of the second victim.

Mr. Estrada described the blood spurting from his neck, and it is completely inconsistent that he would have been able to see that he had ducked and covered as he indicated. All of the other participants in the fracas who testified to related circumstances wherein, none of them saw the second person shot because they all began to scatter. I think the jury's view is that there is only one way that Mr. Estrada could have seen that, and that is because he was looking down the barrel of the gun at the time."[36]

With those words, Judge Ochoa sealed the fate of Tony Estrada. Prior to rendering sentence, the judge asked Lax if the defendant wished to make a statement. Lax looked to Tony, who was sternly nodding yes. Estrada then stood and awkwardly maneuvered himself to face the courtroom gallery, as his legs and hands were now shackled and attached to a chain encircling his waist. Looking into the eyes of the mother of Mitchell Sanchez seated in the front row behind him, he told her:

"I want to say that I am very sorry for what happened, for your loss. I want to let everyone know that I know in my heart that I didn't shoot nobody, and I do believe in letting nature take its way, and I believe that the Lord is going to find the guilty one soon. I pray every day. I pray every day that the Lord will let both of the families know someday that it wasn't me, the one that shot neither one of them. I know in my heart that I didn't do it and the Lord knows that I am not the one that did it neither."

Angela Rodriguez then cried out from the audience, "Tell them who did it, Tony!" Judge Ochoa quickly took control and harshly told her that there were to be no outbursts from the audience, or he would have to remove her from the courtroom. Despite the cries of his mother, Tony Estrada did not answer her. Instead he said,

"And if I was the one that did it, may I burn in Hell, because I know that I didn't do it. And the Lord is right here, right now, listening to what I am saying, and I am telling you guys, I am not the one that shot."[37]

With that, the defense concluded its presentation. Judge Ochoa thanked Estrada for his statement, and then sentenced him to a total term of forty-one years to life in prison. Judge Ochoa's rationale for the sentence was simple. It was a particularly brutal and senseless crime. Beyond that, he was mindful of the fact that the bullet that had struck John Moreno in the neck had missed his aorta by less than a millimeter, barely avoiding a second death. Judge Ochoa explained, "We very easily could have been talking about a death penalty versus life without parole situation because of a multiple murder."[38]

The case of the People v. Tony Estrada was now over. Estrada would file a Notice of Appeal and have a new attorney appointed. The Appellate Court would find no error in his conviction. His case was affirmed on appeal. All that was left was for Tony Estrada to serve out the full term of his life sentence in the California Department of Corrections.

CHAPTER 5

Pelican Bay

SHORTLY AFTER HIS sentencing, Tony Estrada was transferred from the Santa Barbara County Jail to Wasco State Prison in Kern County. At that time, California had four levels of prisons, ranging from low security (level one) to high security (level four). The nature of the inmate's crime, his length of term, prior record, reputation for violence and gang affiliation all go into determining an inmate's prison. In 1985, the total number of prisons in California was thirteen. From 1985 to 1995, an additional eighteen prisons were built to house over 160,000 inmates, making California's the largest state prison system in the country.[39]

Tony Estrada's security evaluation was not difficult to process. He had been convicted of murder in a gang-related crime. His sentence of forty-one years to life virtually assured he would die in prison. Under the criteria, Tony was given a high score for violence with a strong likelihood of association with a prison gang. Since he had no real hope of parole, he would have little motivation to rehabilitate himself. The prison system would be unable to discipline him by taking away "good time" credits for bad behavior. There was little they could do to him, other than what they had already done. Tony Estrada was a high-risk inmate appropriate for a maximum-security prison. Tony was sent to Pelican Bay.

Pelican Bay State Prison sits on two hundred seventy acres of land about ten miles south of the Oregon state border. Originally designed to house 2,280 inmates, at the time of Tony's arrival, its population had swelled to about 3,300.[40] Completed in 1989 at a cost of 217.5 million dollars, Pelican Bay is one of the most modern and secure penal facilities in the country. It is an imposing gray hulk of reinforced concrete devoid of trees and surrounded by razor wire on all sides and observation towers at every corner. Its eight cell blocks radiate from a three-acre exercise yard like the spokes of a wheel.

Located just off the Pacific Ocean, the weather is almost always cold and gloomy. The sky is usually gray or darker, and rarely does sunlight actually break through to touch prison walls. The perpetual gray fog and gray walls of the prison complex seem to blend together to form an oppressive, colorless gloom.

When dedicated by Governor George Deukmejian in 1990, Pelican Bay was described as the nation's most secure prison. Built to isolate and punish the state's most violent felons, its high-tech complex included a security housing unit (SHU) for the most dangerous inmates. By the time Tony arrived prison in April of 1998, over two-thirds of the cells designed for one man now held two. Only the most violent prisoners were kept in the SHU, where they were held in isolation for a total of twenty-two and a half hours out of every twenty-four. These inmates had earned their own cells by committing acts of violence at other prisons, against other inmates or prison guards. It was for the "worst of the worst" that Pelican Bay had been built, and even with all of its high-tech security systems, keeping control of the prisoners proved both difficult and dangerous.[41]

Unfortunately, as the rest of the country became a more integrated society during the 1960's and 1970's, prison life became more segregated. Prisoners increasingly joined prison gangs based upon race. In California's prisons, these gangs were divided into three major racial groups: Caucasian, African-American and Hispanic. Before long, an unstable balance of terror existed among the races in prison. Any act of violence by a member of one race against another required a more violent response. To be in prison without gang affiliation was like being at war alone.

Over time, the influence of prison gangs spread throughout the entire system and then out onto the streets of America. The gang lifestyle, learned in prison, was then released onto the streets of our major cities. In 2002, the phenomenon was so pervasive that one law enforcement survey estimated that in the City of Los Angeles there were 58,000 gang members. Throughout the United States, there were roughly 26,000 street gangs boasting 840,500 total members.[42]

Gang leadership is based entirely upon "respect." "Respect" is earned through repeated acts of violence. Hardcore members function as enforcers for the gang. Failure to join a gang is an act of disrespect, and a youngster can gain respect by attacking a non-member. Any young man living in a neighborhood where there is an active street gang has a major dilemma. He can either chose to be "jumped in" to the gang, which is a ritual beating required for membership, or be "jumped on" every time gang members catch him alone. This is known as gangster health insurance—that is, it is healthier to get jumped in than to keep getting jumped on. Thus, the cycle continues, with the recruitment of new gang members remaining a dynamic force both inside and outside of prison.

In California, criminal street gangs used to be largely isolated in big-city neighborhoods. Over time, however, the gang phenomenon has spread out into smaller cities and counties. Young men sentenced to prison out of counties such as Ventura or Santa Barbara are immediately recruited into prison gangs. Failure to associate with one's own kind in prison is akin to a death sentence. These small-town criminals are schooled in gangsterism by "big homies," and when released they take their education home with them. Therefore, new gangs are formed in communities where they had never been before.

Generally, gangs operate only in their local community. Most often Hispanic gangs fight with other Hispanic gangs, African-American gangs fight with other African-American gangs and Caucasian gangs fight among themselves. Most of these local rivalries come to an end when a gangster reaches prison. A new prisoner has a choice of only a few select prison gangs. If he is Caucasian, he might associate with the "Nazi Low Riders" or "N.L.R.," which is associated with the other "white" prison gangs, the "Skinheads" and the "Aryan Brotherhood."

If he is an African-American, his choice will largely be limited to the "Black Guerrilla Family" or "B.G.F." If he is Hispanic, his affiliation is determined by his area of residence. If he lived north of Fresno, he would likely associate with "La Familia," and if he is from south of Fresno, his choice would be the "Mexican Mafia" or "EME."[43]

Most prisoners never earn enough respect to become "made members" of prison gangs. Rather, they only associate with their ethnic groups and follow the unwritten rules enforced by the most-feared gang members, those known as "shot callers" or "big homies." These prisoners are best described as associate gang members since they have not earned the right to be a "true soldier." The white prisoners not known as Aryan Brotherhood or Nazi Low Rider may be known as "Peckerwoods" or just plain "Woods," whereas Hispanic prisoners from Northern California are called "Norteños" and those from the south are known as "Sureños."

The most disciplined prison gang in California is the Mexican Mafia. Formed in the 1950's, it is the largest and most powerful gang. Respect for the EME extends far beyond prison walls. Even the Federal government has sought to curtail the activities of the Mexican Mafia through a series of RICO prosecutions.[44] These federal prosecutions proved top bosses in the EME engaged in drug trafficking and murder for hire even while incarcerated at Pelican Bay. Remarkably, shot caller inmates had accounts at the prison that were being used to launder money garnered from criminal enterprises outside prison. Despite the success of this prosecution, the Mexican Mafia is as powerful today as it has ever been.

It was this world of prison gangs and high security tactics that Tony Estrada entered in April of 1998. Unfortunately, Pelican Bay's violent reputation was developed not only by the prisoners, but also by some of the prison guards. After a series of riots and questionable deaths in the late 1980's and early 1990's, a federal class action lawsuit was filed on behalf of the prisoners, alleging civil rights violations. In the case of <u>Madrid v. Gomez</u> in 1995, U.S. District Court Judge Thelton Henderson found Pelican Bay's use of force policy and medical care facilities unconstitutional. His judgment included a finding that the prison administration inflicted cruel and unusual punishment on the inmates. Judge Henderson termed the abuses "senseless suffering and sometimes wretched misery" and noted that the prison was the site of "a pattern of needless and officially sanctioned brutality" against the inmates.[45]

The findings of Judge Henderson were reinforced by other legal actions. In 1994, an inmate won a civil settlement of $997,000.00 for third-degree burns he suffered after allegedly being forced into a scalding bath by prison guards.[46] Then in 1998, the FBI began an investigation that led to the indictment of two guards for conspiracy to violate inmates' constitutional rights by using other inmates to assault them. The indictment alleged that the guards would spread a rumor that a particular inmate was a child molester and then place him with inmates who were known to attack sex offenders. In one instance, a prisoner was stabbed to death.

These cases are a few examples of what occurred at Pelican Bay over a prolonged period of time. The safety and control of prisoners is largely dependent upon the goodwill and courage of the prison guards. They operate largely as a law unto themselves, in a world that nobody else cares about.[47] Long-term sentences and budget cuts to rehabilitative programs have left prison administrators with few options other than sheer force to control prison populations.

Thrust into this world, Tony had to learn the rules of prison life as set down not only by the prison administration but also the inmates themselves. Both sets of rules were designed to regulate almost every aspect of his new life and ultimately destroy his individual identity, as the less a man thinks for himself, the easier he is to control.

Due to a series of riots both before and after Tony's arrival, "lockdown" status had become routine. Lockdown meant prisoners stayed in their cells as much as twenty-two and one-half out of every twenty-four hours. Each cell was approximately twelve feet long, eight feet high and maybe eight feet wide. Crammed into this space were two bunk beds, a sink, a toilet, a writing area, some shelves and perhaps a couple of chairs. These "furnishings" were made of stainless steel, and the walls, floor and ceiling consisted of reinforced concrete. The electronically controlled door, also made of steel, only opened once a day. Through it lunch and dinner were served, and occasionally mail or perhaps reading material came sliding through the door.

Living under these conditions, Tony's daily routine began at 6:00 a.m. He spent the first two hours reading, and then an hour exercising. The limited space in his cell meant push-ups, sit ups and leg squats only. After exercising, Tony would take a "shower" in the sink. Between 10:00 a.m. and 12:00 p.m., he would sit at a desk and write letters to friends and family. Sometime after noon, lunch would be served. At about 2:00 p.m., he sat down to draw pencil art until about 4:00 p.m. At 4:35 p.m., he ate dinner and then watched television with his cellmate until 6:30 p.m. Then he performed a series of stretching exercises before being released to the showers. Upon returning to his cell, Tony would read or watch television until 9:00 p.m. Then lights out. A break in this routine only occurred when he might be taken to an exercise area to work out with a few other prisoners. Basically, Tony's routine was always the same, every hour of every day, every single day, for weeks on end, whenever Pelican was in lockdown.

THE YARD

The most dangerous place in prison is the yard. The only place where inmates are allowed to congregate at one time, the ability of the guards to control and supervise them diminishes. This gives some inmates the opportunity to engage in all kinds of illegal activities. For instance, drug deals commonly go down on the yard. In fact, the use of illegal drugs in California prisons has been so prevalent that one study estimated ten percent of the inmates were under the influence of drugs at any one time.[48]

More disturbing, and certainly more dangerous, is the presence of illegal weapons, usually in the form of homemade prison knives or "shanks." The creation and hiding of prison shanks presents a never-ending battle between the prisoners and the guards. Any substance strong enough to be sharpened to the point of piercing human skin has to be controlled in prison.

The most dangerous weapons are made of materials hardest to come by. For instance, a "bone crusher" made of steel is strong and heavy enough to be driven deep into the body. It is reserved for a victim thought to be deserving of a life-threatening assault, such as a known child molester or rapist or a suspected informant or "snitch." The "one hitter," so called because it may only hold up for one stabbing, is produced from more readily available materials. It might be made by melting down a plastic cup into a cylinder, which is then sharpened to a point. Reserved for less serious offenders like someone who has broken the racial code, this inferior weapon sends a message but rarely threatens life. For example, if a new Hispanic inmate accepted a cigarette from a black prisoner, he might be "shanked" with a "one hitter" to restore order.[49]

It is on the prison yard that the shank is most prevalent. The large open space and various exercise facilities, benches and tables provide plenty of hiding places. The potential for large-scale violence and the use of stabbing instruments has caused the prisoners to liken the yard to a Roman gladiator ring. Whenever there is a riot, it is almost always a conflict between rival gangs. The violence might be spontaneous, such as a conflict between two gang members, which escalates into a larger fight as members of both gangs are forced into action. These fights are easier for the guards to contain and ultimately subdue. However, when a riot is a planned event by one gang seeking dominance over another, the guards' ability to control events is stretched to the limit.

A conspiracy to foment a riot can only occur within the leadership structure of a prison gang. Any act of disrespect, as determined by a shot caller, requires a violent response. To be disrespected and not respond is perceived as weakness. A gang leader can respond to an act of disrespect personally or by using a subordinate known as a "soldier." The soldier is usually a younger inmate seeking to "earn his stripes" and become a made member of the gang. By carrying out the orders of a shot caller, the soldier gains respect.

These circumstances would make it seem impossible for an inmate to avoid joining a prison gang. However, a few exceptions to the rule exist. If an inmate has money or reliable drug connections, he might pay a shot caller for protection. The agreement is nothing less than extortion, but even more than on the outside, drugs and money buy influence and protection. Another way an inmate can stay out or drop out of a prison gang is to provide information to the guards. The guards are always looking for intelligence on crimes that have occurred, or more importantly, about to occur. Rarely will prisoners talk to the guards, even if they are assault victims. Unless the guards see the crime committed, their chances of catching the perpetrator are slim. The victim will tell the guards he never saw his assailant. He was attacked from behind, or he covered his face when attacked, so he couldn't see who did it. Everyone knows he is lying, but nothing will persuade him to give up his attacker. This would be snitching, giving the victim what is known as a "snitch jacket," which he wears wherever he goes from then on. No, it is far better for the victim to seek his own justice later on. Better to have just one enemy lurking than to violate the gang code of silence and be known as a prison rat.

Prisoners giving information to the guards who are found out or "burned" have to be placed in administrative segregation or "ad seg." Informing is a dangerous business, and the guards want to use a snitch as long as possible, but once it is clear that a snitch has been burned, they must remove him from the main population. The trick is to get the snitch out before he is found out.

Another more subtle way to avoid getting caught up in a prison gang was the way chosen by Tony Estrada. Tony became a Christian. It would seem absurd to think that trying to live a Christian life in a place like Pelican Bay would lead to a sanctuary of sorts, but, particularly among the Norteños and Soreños, faith is respected and belief in God is honored. Though most gang members do not believe they can live a Christian life themselves, they hang onto some hope of redemption by giving a pass to those who sincerely make the effort. This code of honor has at its foundation a basic tenet of the faith, that even the most wretched of men have the right to try and save their own souls.

Tony's faith made him a "civilian" in the gang wars that raged around him. That is not to say that he never faced danger, as that would deny the cruel reality of Pelican Bay. Still, the shot callers largely left him alone—that is, until one of his Christian friends failed to back up a Mexican prisoner fighting with two black prisoners. One of the big homies told Tony he would have to take care of the guy since he trusted him. Tony spent an agonizing night of fear and indecision before mustering the courage to tell the shot caller he couldn't do the hit. Tony spent the next several weeks expecting to be shanked at any moment, but the attack never came, and he was never asked again. Tony's faith had been proven sincere. He had been willing to risk himself for someone else. Tony had survived and perhaps even carved out a little respect with the shot callers.

Tony had found his place. He would never be a shot caller, and hopefully he would never have to be a soldier. Though danger could come from anywhere, at any time, he had found, at least for the time being, a place where he did not have to participate in the never-ending gang warfare. Unfortunately, even this small measure of safety was too good to be true. The violent reality of Pelican Bay could not ignore any of its prisoners for long.

CHAPTER 6

The Plan

NOT TOO LONG after arriving at Pelican Bay, Tony was assigned a new cellmate. As always, a screening was done to check compatibility. His cellie was an old childhood friend: Jorge "Chucky" Alvarado. Tony and Jorge had gone to the same elementary school in Oxnard. They had played as boys, and though they were never the best of friends, they were part of the same group of kids going through school together.

As they got older and graduated to middle school and then high school, Jorge and Tony saw less of each other. Jorge's family structure was less stable than Tony's. Though Jorge's mother loved and nurtured him, she had to do so alone. Without the help of Jorge's father, Mrs. Alvarado struggled to keep her small family sheltered, clothed and fed. Most of the time, the family lived in small houses or apartments in the least expensive area of Oxnard, La Colonia. On more than one occasion, Jorge wound up living in a homeless shelter or campground. The instability of his home life made Jorge a prime candidate for membership in the Colonia Chiques. Before long, Jorge started getting into trouble at school and with the Oxnard Police Department. Identified as an associate of the Colonia Chiques early on, his involvement in the gang grew, and so did his criminal record. With each new arrest, Jorge's stays in Juvenile Hall grew longer. Life in the Hall became increasingly familiar, and it even had certain advantages over life on the streets of Colonia. First of all, it was safer. Second, everyone inside the Hall was equal. No one had more than anyone else, and many of Jorge's friends were in the Hall. Consequently, Jorge increasingly became embroiled in the criminal justice system.

Tony came from a more stable background. Tony's father was not a participant in his life, but his mother had always provided for her family by working as a secretary at the local naval base. With the help of her new husband, Angela Rodriguez was able to provide a good home for her sons. Under the watchful eye of his ever-vigilant mother, Tony managed to avoid getting caught up in the local street gang. When Tony graduated from high school, he did so without ever having been arrested—no small achievement in his neighborhood. After high school, Tony went into the U.S. Army on a three-year enlistment. With an honorable discharge, Tony returned to Oxnard.

When Tony learned Jorge would be his new cellie, apprehension struck. Despite their childhood friendship, Jorge intimidated Tony. Tony had heard about Jorge's gang banging. Jorge had grown up quickly and earned a reputation as a great street fighter.

Jorge never grew much taller than five feet, eight inches, but he looked as if he were as broad as he was tall. With a huge barrel chest, Popeye arms, and short, powerful legs, Jorge had the build of a boxer. Jorge became fearless as he discovered he could beat anybody in a fistfight. His strength and courage served him well out on the streets. When challenged, Jorge would "box," even when outnumbered, but as he grew older, the fights got uglier. Jorge started picking up knife wounds, which needed stitches. Then came surgery to repair some bullet wounds. By the time Jorge was sentenced to prison, he had been shot at on nine occasions and actually hit three times. One bullet was never removed and could be felt by rubbing the back of his knee. This wound caused no permanent damage.

The same could not be said for the bullet removed from just below his heart. It had ruptured his esophagus and caused permanent damage to the surrounding muscle tissue. This caused Jorge to suffer from involuntary contractions of his esophagus, which could be heard almost rhythmically as a guttural, gulping sound emanating from his torso. Having survived so many street fights with the scars to prove it, Jorge was a legend of sorts in the Colonia. His courage and reputation for never backing down made him a highly respected member of the Colonia Chiques. Since it was not his nature to tell others what to do, Jorge never aspired to be a leader. Rather, Jorge just took care of his own business. Jorge did not go out looking for trouble, but when it came, someone got hurt. Due to his reputation as a fighter and his uncanny survival skills, the gang dubbed Jorge "Chucky." Just as the Chucky doll of Hollywood movie fame kept coming back from the dead to fight again, so did Jorge "Chucky" Alvarado. With such a fitting moniker, everyone knew him as "Chucky" from then on.

Chucky's reputation gave Tony reason to be concerned about his new cellmate. Chucky was serving a sentence of twelve years on three counts of gang-related home invasion robbery. By the time he celled up with Tony, Chucky had already done over seven years of hard time in various level-four prisons.

Tony had another reason to be concerned: Chucky was deeply ingrained in the Mexican Mafia. Though he never graduated to shot caller status, Chucky was an active soldier. Having performed sufficient services over the years, Chucky was allowed to be known as EME. After checking in with the shot callers, Chucky had a tattoo done on his back of an Aztec warrior. Prison tattoos done with crude instruments and ink from regular pens have none of the artistic characteristics of professional tattoos, but they have much greater symbolic value. They immediately identify the bearer as someone who has been to prison, and, in Chucky's case, his tattoo indicated that he was a made member of the Mexican Mafia. Whether in prison or out on the streets, such a tattoo would command instant respect.[50]

As the days turned into weeks and weeks into months, the two cellies came to know each other well. They would talk forever about the old days on the streets of Colonia and share what they heard about their friends. They talked about who was in jail or prison, who had done what, and who had managed to stay out of it all. They also spoke of their families: who had stood by and who had forgotten them. Tony wrote home a lot and received a lot of mail in return, which he shared with Chucky. Chucky, on the other hand, still a player in the Colonia, stayed in touch with the homies on the streets.

With the passage of time, the cellmates came to trust one another. Chucky could see Tony was sincere about his religion, and Tony observed that there was a kinder, gentler side to Chucky, hidden beneath his chiseled and scarred exterior. Chucky even shared some of his plans with Tony.

Dreams for the future can be a dangerous dalliance in prison. To hope for a better life is considered a weakness, and to share it with other inmates can make one vulnerable. An inmate with no hope for release doesn't want to hear about what someone else is going to do when he gets out. A careless comment like this could cause a violent outburst that, in the minds of other prisoners, is justified. However, Chucky knew Tony wouldn't respond that way, and Chucky, being a short-timer, couldn't help but take advantage of Tony's good nature. Although it was often painful for Tony to hear Chucky's plans, he suffered through it, knowing hope for the future helped keep Chucky alive.

Having talked of just about everything else, the day finally came when the conversation turned to the cause of their incarceration. The story behind an inmate's crime, as told by the inmate, remains suspect even to other prisoners. Somehow, virtually everyone in prison is wrongfully convicted. Therefore, it was of no surprise to Tony that Chucky felt he was innocent. He told Tony he didn't participate in the robbery and that he had no idea what the homeboys were going to do when they entered the house. He didn't have a weapon, and he really didn't do anything—he was just sort of there. However, with his prior record, and because he was Colonia, his case was prosecuted as a gang crime. Chucky had refused to deal; he went down fighting in front of a Ventura County jury. It didn't take them long to convict him of everything. After that, a stiff sentence of twelve years was a foregone conclusion.

Then it was Tony's turn. He had not spoken to anyone about Lot 10 since he testified at trial. By now, he knew he had hurt himself badly. He had wanted to declare his innocence and deny shooting the gun, but he also didn't want to finger anyone else. So, he told the jury he didn't do it, he didn't know who had done it, and he didn't know who else was there when it happened. Since Tony had lied in certain parts of his testimony, the jury didn't believe the rest. Tony had finally concluded he could never tell only half the truth again.

In telling Chucky the truth, Tony was taking a huge risk. He knew that Chucky was ganged up not only with the Mexican Mafia but also the Colonia Chiques. Chucky had run with all the homeboys in Lot 10 before he came to prison. Tony also knew that Chucky had run with Tony's cousin, Alfonso "Capper" Rodriguez. Tony knew if he told Chucky the truth, Chucky might conclude that Tony was ready to give up the other homies in Lot 10 to save himself. If Chucky wanted to, he could burn Tony as a snitch, not only back home on the streets of Colonia, but worse, within the prison walls of Pelican Bay. By telling Chucky everything, Chucky would know how it all went down. However, Tony had come to trust Chucky, so he decided to take a chance.

Tony started off by telling how his girlfriend, Veronica Mendez, had found a babysitter that night so they could go out on the town. Veronica came over early in the evening to Tony's place, a small house in Oxnard that he shared with his cousin Rochelle Gomez and her husband Mauricio. The house was owned by Tony's mother, Angela Rodriguez.

At the house, they met up with Capper and his wife, Monica. From there, they went to dinner at a local Mexican restaurant, where they each had several margaritas. After dinner, they returned home and made plans to go to a nightclub in Santa Barbara. There, they were joined by Carolyn Wright and her boyfriend, Dino Ramirez, and Dino's friend, Gilberto Zapata.

When it was time to leave for Santa Barbara, Tony's cousin Michelle and her husband decided to stay home. When they left, Tony and Veronica rode with Capper and Monica, with Monica driving their black Ford Mustang. Gilberto, Dino and Carolyn followed the Mustang in Carolyn's black Honda Civic. Before getting on the freeway, both cars stopped at a liquor store to buy forty-ounce bottles of Old English malt liquor for the forty-five minute drive north. They drank the beer on the way and discarded the bottles along the freeway—ready to party by the time they reached Santa Barbara.

On arrival, both cars were parked on the second level of Lot 10. Leaving together, the group walked to State Street, where they found the Hurricane Club. They waited a short time outside before paying the five-dollar cover charge and going inside.

Here, Tony had to tell Chucky that his memory of events inside the club was poor. Tony was drunk when he got there, and he continued drinking inside. He did remember they met up with Alfonso Martinez and his girlfriend. Tony also remembered going to the bathroom with Capper and things already being underway with the East Side homeboys when they returned.

As usual, Gilberto was the instigator, despite being badly outnumbered. Seeing the odds, Capper stepped in front of Gilberto and apologized for his smaller, hotheaded friend. Gilberto stepped aside, as he knew he must, and everything seemed cool until the bouncers got involved. Gilberto got crazy again, challenging East Side to a fight outside as he was ushered out the front door.

Outside, at the front of the Hurricane, Tony remembered Gilberto being literally hopping mad. Looking back through a large picture window, Gilberto kept jumping up and down, trying to get a reaction from East Side. Gilberto finally got their attention by throwing gang signs. East Side's reaction caught the attention of the bouncers, so they go thrown out the back.

Everyone from Colonia was now outside in front of the Hurricane, except Alfonso Martinez and his girlfriend, who had managed to avoid the bouncers. A short conversation ensued about what to do before heading home to Oxnard. Deciding to leave, they all started walking back to Lot 10. Dino was out in front with Carolyn, followed closely by Gilberto, and then Tony and Veronica. Bringing up the rear were Capper and Monica. As they approached the parking lot, there were the East Side homeboys; Michael Chavez, who had started the trouble inside, once again moved in on Carolyn. Rather than fight, Dino took off running.

Gilberto was not so easily intimidated. Still enraged about being thrown out of the club, he couldn't wait to fight. Sprinting forward, Gilberto grabbed a bicycle leaning against a tree. Twisting his body around in a circle, he launched it high into the air at East Side while screaming "Colonia." The bike landed short, but East Side wasn't about to let it ride. Spreading out in a circle, East Side quickly came up behind Tony and Veronica, pushing them into Lot 10.

At this point, Tony had to admit he was very much afraid. They were outnumbered at least five to one, and they were surrounded. Tony looked around frantically for Capper, but he was nowhere to be found. A deafening chant of "East Side" echoed throughout the parking lot as the circle around them continued to close. Tony saw a beer bottle fly past his head, and then he heard it shatter against the pavement.

Then, just as East Side surged forward for their final assault, Tony noticed Capper out of the corner of his eye. Walking straight at the advancing homeboys of East Side, Tony could see light reflecting from the surface of the steel-plated revolver in his hand. The gun looked enormous and the sight of it terrified him, but that was nothing compared to the horror he felt when the first shots were fired. The explosions flashed from behind his right shoulder, and the thunder that followed made him duck. Tony screamed "Noooo," but his cry was destroyed by another explosion from the gun.

Tony told Chucky about seeing the first homeboy fall. He had been out front leading the pack, just as Capper came up from behind. The bullet hit him squarely in the neck, stopping him in his tracks. Clutching his neck, Tony saw a trail of blood seep through his hands before he fell straight over backward to the pavement below, his knees refusing to buckle.

Gripped with fear, Tony could only watch as Capper stalked past him. More explosions lit the garage as Capper pursued the panicked homeboys scattering in front of him. Capper took careful aim, squeezing off another round. Thunder again pounded the concrete as Capper continued his lesson on respect and what it meant to be a real gangster.

As the memory of Mitchell Sanchez came into focus, Tony had to turn away from Chucky, blinking back tears of sorrow he thought he had long since buried. Sanchez came into view as he turned to run from the middle of the pack. He had gotten off a stride or two when he suddenly lurched forward, his feet losing contact with the ground, just as a .38 caliber slug caught him in the back of the head. He hit the pavement face first. Tony hoped he had merely tripped and that he would soon gather himself to rise and run again. All hope faded as Tony saw streams of red pulsating down both sides of his neck, collecting in an ever-growing pool beneath his head. Still, Capper was not satisfied; he continued hunting them, firing the last two shots at their backs as they ran away. With the last of the gunshots and their echoes finally drifting away, the garage finally fell still. Tony could smell smoke as he recalled how the lingering haze of spent gunpowder permeated the garage.

Tony remained frozen in place as Capper turned and ran past him, hesitating just long enough to pass the revolver to Gilberto. Gilberto was now in possession of the longed-for instrument of supreme power. Taking it in his right hand, he ran to John Moreno, who was lying face up on the pavement, and stopped, bent down slightly, placed the barrel of the gun to his head and pulled the trigger. Tony closed his eyes, unable to watch anymore. Hearing nothing, Tony opened his eyes to see Gilberto hitting Moreno with the gun on each side of his face, causing his head to snap violently back and forth with the landing of each new blow.

Tony then heard Dino screaming something at Mitchell Sanchez as Sanchez lay face down, bleeding on the concrete. Tony clutched his stomach as Dino kicked away at Sanchez's lifeless body. Dino struck with such a force that Tony could see blood spatter up into the air, until finally a brown, thicker substance came oozing out the back of Sanchez's head onto the cement below. Transfixed by the horror of it all, Tony remained unable to move or make a sound. It seemed to Tony that Gilberto and Dino would never be satisfied. Each new blow was recorded in slow motion in Tony's memory, having been wound and rewound for viewing countless times.

Then just as suddenly as it started, it ended. Without a word, both Gilberto and Dino took off running for the front exit. Tony had the urge to run after them, but still he was unable to make himself move.

Tony watched in agony as the pools of blood beneath Moreno and Sanchez kept growing. They looked strangely familiar to him. About his age and size, they wore the same clothes and hairstyles that he and his friends did. Tony longed to help, to go to them, to somehow undo what had been done, but the trauma of it all had rendered him paralyzed. He remained stupefied, unable to help the young men bleeding to death before him.

Chucky noticed Tony's voice trailing off as he described the final scene. Silence lingered between the cellmates until Chucky, in irritation, asked, "Well what happened, how'd you get busted?" Tony, brought back to the present, thought for a moment and realized he had no memory of his arrest. The events of Lot 10 after the shooting he reported to Chucky from his memory of the trial.

Realizing what he had now done, Tony held his breath and waited for Chucky to respond. Chucky said nothing, showing no emotion as he sat stiffly on the side of his bunk. Tony was close to panic, afraid he had given himself up or that Chucky would never believe him. All the institutionalized "paranoia of the prisoner" attacked Tony inside his head. He thought what little was left of his life was now over. It would be only a matter of time before someone walked up behind him in the shower and shanked him in the neck, or three prisoners caught him alone in the day room, or death came in the middle of the night while he lay sleeping.

Finally Chucky broke the silence. "I always thought it was Capper," he said indignantly. "Most everyone thinks he did it. Some people thought it might be Gilberto, but I always knew Capper did it. Capper's a killer; Gilberto's just stupid."

Tony, startled, gathered himself, asking, "How come you never told me, if that's what you think? Man, why didn't you tell me?"

"Hey, it's your business, dog. I figured you'd let me know sooner or later, but I wasn't going to get involved in your situation unless you wanted it."

Tony hesitated, digesting Chucky's indifference, and then challenged, "What makes you so sure that it wasn't me? How do you know I'm not bullshitting, just like everyone else in here?"

Chucky laughed a short, cruel laugh. "Oh, hell. Tony everybody knows you ain't got the balls for nothing like that."

Tony didn't know whether to be pleased or offended, but after consideration, he realized that Chucky had only spoken the truth.

Chucky went on, "You know, I was with Capper more than once when he pulled that shit. One time, we were all going to go to this party in Oxnard, but they didn't want to let us in, you know, because we were Colonia, and they didn't want any fights. Well, Capper was drunk of course. Capper's always loaded on something. So we're at the front gate hassling these guys, gettin' it going, and Capper, he doesn't say nothin', he just turns and walks away, back to his van. But me and the other homies, we're there, still trying to get us in, talkin' shit and gettin' ugly, when all of a sudden, I hear gunshots behind me, and there's Capper, running at us, blastin' away. He didn't care. Capper doesn't give a fuck. It scared me, dog, so I take off running, and I ain't looking back—I ain't getting' shot again, especially by that fool."

The more Chucky remembered, the more indignant he became. "That's Capper alright, driving 'round Oxnard, all drunk and coked up, in that pretty van of his, always a revolver hidden in back, case some shit is goin' down."

Up out of his bunk, getting worked up, Chucky started pacing back and forth the short distance of the cell. Tony looked down on Chucky from the top bunk with amusement. Then Chucky let it go: "You know, it ain't right, man. It just ain't right. That's bullshit, man—letting another homie, your own blood man, your primo, do your time for you. That shit ain't right, dog."

Enjoying Chucky's antics, Tony asked, "What's up with that, Chucky?"

"I mean that's low, man, fucking bullshit, you serving his time. It ain't right, it just ain't right," Chucky growled, slamming his fist into his open hand for emphasis. "Capper's a chicken shit, man. Capper don't even box no mo', used to when he was a kid, got a big Johnny-bad-ass reputation cause he was bigger than everybody, but not no more, just bang, bang, bang, run away. What a chicken shit, dog, a piece of shit." Chucky's pace had increased and the muscles in his chest, back and arms tightened as if preparing for a fight.

Tony didn't like when Chucky got like this; it was more than a little scary. But Tony also sensed he was going somewhere with this when he abruptly shifted. "What's going on with your appeal, man? Ain't you got somethin' still going?"

The mention of his appeals skidded Tony back to Earth. His first appeal to the local Court of Appeals had been unanimously denied.[51]

His request for review to the California Supreme Court was also denied. Tony had exhausted all his appeals, and the judgment in his case stood final. With obvious sadness, Tony admitted, "It's over. My appeals are all over."

Chucky again slammed his fist into his palm and belched, one of his spontaneous guttural belches, and then snorted like a bull. Chucky was mad, very mad, but he managed to keep his anger under control. Chucky had blown it big time, and he knew it. Chucky had seen other men refuse to give up hope, even though, like Tony, they had no chance of release, eventually driving themselves crazy with such foolishness. Some would lose touch with reality altogether, constantly babbling about their latest appeal and how they were sure to win this time. They held on only to be crushed again, either by the system or the lies their own minds had told them. These were the weakest of men in prison, perpetual victims, doomed to fall prey to the cruelest inmates who would amuse themselves by pretending to listen and then taunting them with reality, forcing them to confront their delusions. Sometimes, they would even beat the madness out of the weaklings, only to have them come back from the infirmary more deluded than ever, to the continuing amusement of their tormentors.

No, Chucky would not play mind games with Tony. He would not encourage him to hope—it was too dangerous. So, without saying another word, Chucky finished his pacing and dove into the lower bunk. Neither man spoke again that night, but neither man slept, either. Tony was engaged in a great struggle to think of anything other than the possibility he might someday be released from prison. Being of strong mind and character, Tony ultimately succeeded in returning to reality.

Chucky's mind, on the other hand, foamed into a frenzy. He was angry with himself; he had stepped over the line, and he knew better, but he couldn't let it go. The thought of Tony doing Capper's time enraged him. Capper was letting his homie—no, worse, his primo, his own flesh and blood—rot in prison for a crime he didn't do. Capper violated Chucky's sense of honor, putting in motion the very powerful wheels of Chucky's mind.

The next morning, things were awkward between the cellmates. Both men went about their morning routines with barely a word spoken. When the cell door finally opened, they went their separate ways, first to their jobs, and later out onto the yard.

That evening, after lock up, things loosened up a bit. Tony's case was never spoken of again. Ultimately, things returned to normal—until one night a few weeks later then Chucky had a little surprise for his friend.

Chucky had been working on it for a while, and he felt he owed it to Tony to share it. Chucky had taken some raisins, a little old fruit, and a few packs of sugar, and, following an ancient prison recipe, fermented them in a large plastic bag he kept carefully hidden. Now, his efforts had come to fruition, and a very sweet and pungent bottle of "Pruno" was uncorked.

Chucky, never much of a drug user, liked a good drink once in a while. Tony hadn't drunk since the night of his arrest almost four years earlier, but after lights out, they both enjoyed Chucky's most recent vintage in the privacy of their cell.

As the night wore on and they continued to relax, the conversation again turned toward home. Tony began by telling Chucky that his mother and aunt were still working on his case. They were raising money to hire a lawyer, but they couldn't say what the lawyer might do.

Chucky listened to Tony explain himself for a long time. When Tony finished, he waited a moment and then said softly, "I wrote Capper a letter." Tony, startled, gathered himself to ask, "About what?"

Now almost whispering, Chucky said, "I told him you and I are cellies, and you'd been talkin' about how your case was comin' back on appeal, and this time you weren't goin' to take the fall for him, and that you'd been talkin' all kinds of shit, 'bout how he should be here instead of you; scared him pretty good."

Tony said nothing, so Chucky kept going. "So Capper wrote back, told me to call him, so I did, and we talked about his situation."

Tony didn't like the sound of this. "What are you doing, Chucky, trying to get me killed or something? You're crazy, Chucky, you're losing it, man." Chucky laughed a short, sinister laugh and belched from the gut. Then in a lower, harsher tone, he said, "What do you care, Tony? You're already dead anyway. Besides, I'll probably be the one that gets it, not you, so just shut the fuck up."

Chucky waited to see if Tony showed proper respect and then added, "Capper's freaking out, he's all paranoid and shit on the phone. So I ask him if he wants me to take care of his situation, and he says 'how much?' So I tell him it's going to cost him; I tell him a couple quarters, one smack, one cocaine and twenty bucks on my books. So today I get this money order receipt in the mail, showing twenty dollars on my books." With that, Chucky tossed the folded receipt up to Tony in the top bunk, saying, "See, Tony, see what your life's worth in here."[52]

Tony slowly unfolded the receipt. Just as Chucky said, a money order for twenty dollars made payable to Jorge Alvarado, paid for by Alfonso Rodriguez, stared back at him. Stunned, Tony could only mumble, "What are you doing, Chucky? I don't get it." Chucky laughed louder and meaner than ever, and then waited, obviously enjoying Tony's distress.

Tony tried again. Trembling, he asked, "Chucky, why are you doing this?"

Chucky, further amused by Tony's pitiful plea, again raised the level of hostility. "Shut the fuck up, Tony. You don't know shit about anything. Keep your mouth shut and listen up, dog."

Chucky hesitated, and Tony knew to stay quiet, but he also sensed that Chucky's tirade lacked sincerity. Finally, Chucky spoke, this time in a deadly serious tone. "I'm going to take him down, Tony. I don't care what I have to do—I'm going to take Capper down. I can't take it, man, that shit ain't right, dog, letting your primo do your time for you. That's all fucked up man, so I'm going to take him down, if I can. I don't care what I have to do—I'll wear a wire, I'll do anythin' the man tells me to, but I'm going to take Capper down. I can't live with it no more."

Tony reeled, not knowing what to believe. He knew Chucky was talking stupid. Chucky snitching off Capper! The more he thought of it, the crazier it became, and Tony didn't need any more trauma in his life. Tony decided to put an end to Chucky's latest adventure. "You're crazy, Chucky—out of your mind crazy—and I don't want to hear any more of your bullshit, man."

Chucky laughed again, but not as hard or loud as before, saying, "I can't stop it now, Tony. I'm already inside his head, and I wouldn't stop it now, even if I could. You see, Capper thinks I'm going to take care of his problem. You're already bought and paid for, Tony, and if he doesn't believe that I've taken care of it, he'll have to make other arrangements."

A chill ran down Tony's spine. Chucky was right; he was always right, dead right. Chucky had told Capper Tony was talking shit about him. Even if Chucky burned Capper and didn't do the hit, Capper couldn't afford to let it go. He wouldn't let it go. He would have to take care of business, and it wouldn't take Capper long to find someone inside Pelican to do it for him. The place was literally filled with murderers. Tony was trapped in a world created for him, first by Capper and now by Chucky. The thought of it made him angry, but he couldn't afford to stay mad for long. Besides, Chucky was right—he was dead, dead and buried inside a reinforced concrete tomb. So what if Capper had him stabbed in the neck one day? Death was one of the only ways out of Pelican, and he had no reason to live. "So what if Chucky is crazy?" Tony thought, "My life is nothing. I have nothing to lose." Gathering himself, Tony said softly, "So what's up, Chucky? What are you up to now?"

Chucky was pleased; he hadn't been sure how Tony would react. He also knew that the idea was very dangerous, not just to the body but to the mind, which was much worse. Chucky could live with the threat of being attacked—he always had—but could Tony? He thought he could even live in prison with a snitch jacket on if he had to, but he didn't know if Tony could survive in prison, hanging onto the hope of some crazy scheme. He knew his friend was stronger than he looked, much stronger, but he wasn't sure anybody was that strong. But Chucky couldn't stop himself; some force deep within him was driving him on. He had to make it right. He had to bring Capper down, and maybe, just maybe, he might help out his friend.

Besides, he had already put his plan into motion, and Capper had taken the bait just like Chucky knew he would. Now, he had to explain himself and his plan to Tony. Tony, having accepted that he was no longer alive, was ready to hear it. So Chucky began, "You see, we can set him up, Tony. Capper's a punk—he don't know nothing about the mind games that go on here in prison. He's never been to the joint. Capper's a punk, a big fat punk who thinks he's tough, but he ain't shit, and that's why we can play him. Hell, I'm already inside his head."

Tony was listening intently; he knew Chucky was some kind of prison genius.

"All we got to do is to get him to believe I've taken care of his problem—you know, that I stuck you one night, something like that, then I'll own him! Then, we'll tell him that you were hurt, hurt bad, went to the hospital, and all that shit, and that you're scared, real scared of big bad Capper, who's got such a long reach that he got to you in Pelican Bay. He'll believe it—he'll want to believe a big homie like he is can take you out anytime he wants to. So, you'll let it be known back in Oxnard that you've been hurt, or just say you've been sick or somethin', and that you were in the hospital. Capper's sure to hear about it, and then he'll know I've taken care of his situation here. Then I'll own him. He'll be all grateful and shit, and feel like a real gangster, and believe I'm his homie on the inside."

With that, Chucky stood up, slapped his hands together and turned quickly around in the cell like a dancer, followed by a wicked laugh and a short belch.

Chucky's glee over working Capper was fun for Tony, but Tony didn't get it. "So what, Chucky, so what if you're in his head like that, so he sends you money or whatever, what's up with that?"

Chucky looked indignant. "You're such a dumb shit sometimes, Tony. Don't you know nothin', after how long you've been down here? Don't you see, he'll trust me, man. He'll tell me anythin', so all I got to do is set him up. Some cowboy in Oxnard wants Capper, wants him bad, gotta be someone at old Oxnard P.D. that wants Capper off the streets, and we'll give' em Capper on a stake. Fuck, man, yah know they want Capper, they want him real bad. Hell, we'll make some punk detective into a fucking captain or somethin'." With that, Chucky returned to his bunk and slowly sat down to think it through a little more.

It had started to sound pretty good to Tony, like Chucky could make it happen, but the next step in the plan was the hard one, the impossible one. Who at Oxnard P.D., or anywhere for that matter, listens to what a couple of cons in Pelican Bay have to say about anything? Chucky may have been a major player in the Colonia, but he'd been gone for seven years, and Tony was nobody. The thought that anyone, let alone a police detective, would ever take anything they had to say seriously was ridiculous.

Pelican Bay's ever-present cloud of doom and despair made its way back into their cell. How could they ever get someone in law enforcement to listen to them? They were ancient history, convicts with no credibility and every reason to lie. Tony's story was just another variation of the same old story told by convicts everywhere: "I'm innocent, and some other dude did it."[53] A prolonged silence descended upon their conversation.

However, the fire burning inside Chucky was not easily put out. After thinking a moment longer, Chucky broke the silence with a promise. "I'm going to make it happen, Tony. No matter what, it's going to happen."

Tony was shocked as the impact of what Chucky said hit him. Chucky could say it was something else, he could say it was because he didn't like Capper, or that he didn't like what Capper did, or it "just ain't right," but Tony realized that Chucky would do it, and he would do it for him. Chucky would ruin his status in prison, destroy his reputation on the streets and risk his life for Tony. Only for Tony. Overwhelmed, Tony didn't know what to do or think, but then a thought came into his mind . . . no, not a thought, but a memory of something he recently read: "Greater love hath no man than this, that a man lay down his life for his friends."[54]

Now he remembered, it was from The Bible, but it seemed so out of place when thinking of Chucky. Tony thought a lot of his friend, but a saint he was not.

Confusion reigned in Tony's mind as so many conflicting thoughts and emotions battled for control. Then, Tony knew what he had to do, and it was the only thing he could do. With unusual strength and conviction in his voice, Tony asked, "Chucky, will you pray with me?" Chucky didn't say a word; he didn't know what to say. Praying wasn't something he did. "If there is a God, he's never done nothin' for me, no way, no how, not about to start now."

Tony climbed down from the top bunk, got down on his knees on the concrete floor facing Chucky, and folded his hands together, leaning his elbows against the mattress. Only out of respect for his friend,

Chucky turned to sit on the side of the bunk, putting his feet on the floor. Tony looked up and Chucky nodded softly back.

Then Tony prayed out loud. He prayed for Chucky, he prayed for their families, he prayed for a miracle, he prayed for justice; not just justice in the eyes of man, but justice in the eyes of God.

To anyone who might have seen or heard his prayer knowing their circumstances, it surely would have been a pitiful sight. The thought that anyone in a position of power would ever see or listen to what they had to say was absurd. But for now, it was all very real. No longer were they just a couple of cons locked in a cell deep inside a concrete tomb living out meaningless lives of total despair. For the moment at least, they were nothing less than God's children, bold and unafraid, and filled with hope for the future.

CHAPTER 7

No Regrets

AFTER FORMING THE plan, Tony and Chucky began living a different life in prison. It was a secret life contained completely within their own minds.

To reveal their new life would be stupid. Just to believe in it posed a danger. On the outside, Tony and Chucky went about their daily routines as if nothing had changed. Maintaining the appearance of sanity was essential to the success of their insane plan.

In compliance with the plan, Tony soon let it be known he had spent some time in the infirmary. The dissemination of this information onto the streets of Oxnard was carefully prepared. Tony quit writing in order to raise concerns among his regular correspondents. Since Tony responded to anyone who wrote him, his failure to write back caused immediate concern. Then, after collecting two or three letters of inquiry from the regulars, Tony finally responded in vague terms, and his explanation was the same for everyone. He told them he had been sick but he was better now, and there was nothing to worry about. When pressed for details, Tony either ignored the request or insisted he was fine and that it should just be forgotten.

The disinformation portion of the plan had the desired effect upon its intended audience. Capper contacted Chucky by mail shortly after news of Tony's sickness hit the streets. Capper showed his appreciation to Chucky by carefully concealing a couple of gifts he sent to him upon hearing of Tony's misfortune. Also, within the package was a letter written in coded language seeking details of Tony's near-fatal experience.

Chucky's response to Capper was, as always, well calculated and measured. Ignoring any opportunity to thank Capper for the gifts, Chucky launched an attack for "talking like a fool" and being "stupid." He didn't know what he was talking about, and if he did, he would never be so stupid as to put it in a prison letter. Chucky's response even expressed a note of panic, unusual for Chucky. To a sophisticated ex-con, Chucky's letter would have been made as over the top. But for Capper, it was a perfect manipulation. Nothing from Chucky could have convinced Capper more of the truth of Tony's demise.

Unfortunately, there was an unintended backlash for Tony. Just as Capper had assumed Tony had been hit, so did Tony's family—most especially, his mother.

Angela Rodriguez's emotional wound over the loss of her son was torn open again. She communicated her distress to Tony as only a mother could. Not only was Tony sentenced to life in prison, but now his life was in jeopardy. Writing Tony, she let him know she would not rest until she had found a lawyer who could set him free, no matter what the cost.

Tony, beside himself with guilt, felt he should have known how painful it would be for his mother. She had never given up, and now she had made his rescue her life's work. Tony's remorse was more than he could bear. Despite Chucky's vigorous and sometimes threatening objections, Tony wrote his mother to come visit. Angela Rodriguez drove to Pelican Bay from Oxnard the next weekend.

Angela hated visiting Tony in prison. When corresponding, it was possible to think he was just away from home like when he was in the army. But seeing Tony wearing standard prison issue, behind the thick glass partition keeping her from the slightest touch of his hand, remained a stark brutal reminder of his fate. Though a strong and loving mother, Angela knew her limitations. She knew, and Tony whole-heartedly agreed, that it was not good for them to see each other like this.

However, today was different. As she waited behind the glass for the heavy metal door to slowly roll open, Angela felt a sense of excitement. When at last Tony appeared, Angela could no longer contain her enthusiasm. Finally, she could see he was all right. He bore no visible injuries, no visible scars. He was a little skinnier and clearly lighter of skin, but still in one piece. Angela's relief at seeing her son caused her to break into a great smile. Her eyes, reflecting the strong overhead lighting, revealed small tears forming at the edges.

The happiness in his mother's face caught Tony by surprise. Normally, she carried herself through these encounters with quiet dignity. Seeing her joy, Tony could not help but respond with a little smile of his own, an outward display of emotion he rarely allowed himself.

As Tony approached the glass partition, both of them reached for the telephone receivers hanging from hooks attached to the wall dividing the booths on either side. Tony began by asking how his family and particularly his little brother were getting along. Now in high school, Brian had outstanding grades and was the pride of the family. If he kept it up, Brian would be the first to make it into college, a dream his mother had worked hard and saved for since he was a baby. Tony had always loved and cared for Brian, and he was grateful he was a source of comfort to their mother. After discussing Brian's latest successes, Angela told Tony his other cousin, Rochelle Gomez, had moved out of the front house along with her husband, Mauricio and the baby. They both had taken jobs in New Mexico. They didn't like the weather compared to Oxnard, but they felt it was a safer place to raise a family.

Tony understood what his mother was telling him. Capper again. Capper knew his cousin, Rochelle, and her husband, Mauricio, were potential witnesses against him. Though they had not gone to Santa Barbara the night of the shooting, and when later questioned they said nothing, Capper took no chances.

Tony heard Capper had instructed some of the little homies in Colonia to carry out an intimidation campaign against his cousin's family. Little gangsters were hanging out on the street corner in front of their home, and whenever they came out, all the homeboys would stop what they were doing and stare. This was known as "mad dogging," and it was done with such menace that its purpose was obvious. Mauricio Gomez, being a former Marine, did not suffer the indignity well. Seeing them, he would taunt the "new punks in the neighborhood" about how they would never fight someone "man to man," and he claimed that he "could kill a punk with his bare hands if he wanted to." This always bought a desperate plea from Rochelle, begging her husband not to antagonize them.

Tony also heard that the harassment had recently escalated to nighttime raids. Mauricio, Rochelle and their baby would awake in the middle of the night to the sound of rocks and bottles hitting the windows and the screeching of tires as the wannabes made their getaway. Mauricio knew better than to call the police. About the time Mauricio decided he would have to go to the source of the problem, Rochelle announced her desire to move to New Mexico.

The thought of Capper and his recent attack on his cousin's family brought Tony back to why he had summoned his mother to Pelican Bay. The expression on his face grew serious as he contemplated just how to tell his mother about the plan. He knew she would be totally in favor of anything that might free him, despite the danger involved. His mother wanted her son back, and no threat would scare her off. She would never give up hope. Finally, when his mother finished telling him about his cousin's new home, Tony waited a moment and then said, "Mom, I have something I have to tell you, but you must promise not to speak a word of it to anyone." Angela nodded yes and grew quiet, which was sign enough for Tony. "You see, Mom, Chucky and I have come up with a plan, a plan to give Alfonso up, and maybe even get us out of here."

Angela could not contain her enthusiasm. "Oh, that's wonderful Mijo! Oh, thank you, thank you." Tears once again filled her eyes. She had not heard anything yet, but it was the first time since his conviction Tony had offered his mother any hope at all. For Angela, anything was better than nothing, and she had been living with nothing for a very long time.

His mother's reaction made Tony nervous. He did not want to draw attention to their conversation, so he scolded her, "Calm down, Mom, you can't let on to anyone that something is up." Angela, chastised, caught herself as Tony hesitated. "So Chucky—you remember Chucky from the old neighborhood—he's pretty smart, always was," to which Angela nodded in agreement, even though she didn't agree at all. "Well, he's got a plan, you see, and he's inside Alfonso's head, you know, he's gotten Alfonso to trust him."

Tony, barely speaking above a whisper, had Angela straining to understand. "He got inside Alfonso's head by telling him I was going to be coming back to court on appeal or something, only this time I was going to give him up, so Chucky told Capper that he would take care of me, for him—you know, he would hit me, or stab me or something." This part Angela had no trouble believing about Chucky, as she always knew he was trouble. She had tried with some success to keep Tony away from Chucky, and now she knew why.

"So anyway," Tony continued, "that's why we had to make everyone think something bad had happened to me, like I'd been hurt or something, so that Alfonso would believe Chucky had done a hit on me But you see, Mom, it never happened; it was just a story we made up for Alfonso."

A look of relief came over Angela's face, which then slowly turned to anger. How could Tony have let her think he had been hurt? Didn't he know how she would feel? Tony heard the anger growing in her voice as Angela demanded, "How could you have let me think that, Tony? Do you know what I've been through these past few weeks, worrying about you? And now you tell me you made the whole thing up!" Angela sat back and folded her arms across her chest, waiting for an answer.

Tony had anticipated her reaction, and he knew what would ensure her forgiveness. "We had to do it that way, Mom. You had to believe it so Alfonso would believe it, too."

Angela's demeanor softened as she saw the reason for her suffering. Besides, suffering over a man she loved and believing his lies was nothing new for Angela. What could she do, other than what she had always done? She quickly forgave Tony and allowed him to continue uninterrupted.

"So you see, Mom, Chucky's got Alfonso right where he wants him. Alfonso thinks Chucky is his man on the inside, so if Chucky ever has the chance to talk to Alfonso—you know, when someone is listening, or better yet, tape recording it—maybe he could get Alfonso to admit that he did the shooting." With that, Tony leaned back and waited for a response.

Angela thought, "That's it, that's the plan? Don't they know they are locked up six hundred miles from Oxnard where Alfonso is still running the streets?" Then she caught herself, forcing her mind to stop doubting. This plan was all they had, and she needed to believe in something. She committed herself: "Is there anything, anything at all, I can do to help?" Tony, pleased with his mother's submissive response, replied, "Well, I don't think so, Mom, other than don't mess it up by letting anyone else know, O.K.?" Angela let this latest display of disrespect go by, meekly answering, "O.K., son."

Tony sensed her disappointment. "The problem we have is getting some cop we can trust to listen to our story."

"Oh, is that all?" thought Angela, but then caught herself, saying, "Well, I used to know a couple of those Oxnard cowboys in my day. Perhaps I can persuade one of them to help." A sly smile crossed Angela's lips, one that her son didn't altogether approve of, but Tony knew he needed all the help he could get, no matter how he got it.

The message had now been conveyed in full, so Tony saw no reason to risk further disclosure. Abruptly he changed the subject: "How was the drive up from Oxnard?" Angela lied again, saying, "It was beautiful, Mijo." The conversation then turned to more pleasant topics about good times in the past—a repetitious but emotionally safe discussion.

It wasn't long before Angela got the sense it was time to go. Tony had said what he wanted to say, and he wasn't good at small talk. Angela wanted to stay longer, just to know, for the time being at least, that he was safe, but she knew not to ask of Tony more than he could give. She lingered a bit before telling him it was time to go. Tony abruptly stood, hung the phone on the wall, and started to turn away. As he did, Angela jumped to her feet and banged twice on the glass, and then held her hand spread out on the window. Tony reluctantly turned back to his mother, and placed his hand upon the glass, opposite hers. Angela softly mouthed the words, "I love you, Mijo," through the glass. Tony couldn't hear the words, but he knew them just the same. Tony nodded slightly and then slowly turned toward the steel door leading back into the depths of Pelican Bay. Reaching the door, Tony placed his hands behind his back and waited for it to open. Angela watched her son through the glass for what seemed like a very long time. Finally, she heard the sound of the lock banging open, and the steel door slowly rolled open. Angela watched as a guard appeared and stood behind Tony. Tony then marched forward, never looking back.

<hr />

That evening, back in their cell, things were not going well between Tony and Chucky. Tony kept quiet, preferring to avoid a confrontation. Chucky needed to know Tony hadn't defied him. Tony's silence made it apparent to Chucky that Tony had told his mother everything. Finally, Chucky could take no more. "So you told her, didn't you?" Tony hesitated a moment, searching for words, but only managed "That's right." Chucky jumped out of the lower bunk and started pacing, as he always did when angered.

"You're a punk, Tony, a fucking punk. That's why you're here man, 'cause you always punk out." Tony remained placid, having prepared himself for the worst. "If I end up wearing a snitch jacket, and the whole thing turns to shit, it's on you, Tony, you got me?" and with that Chucky let out a short belch and jumped back into his bunk.

Tony knew what Chucky was telling him. Chucky had decided on a course of action. Tony, gathering himself, said firmly, "I'm alright with that, Chucky."

Rage passed through Chucky's mind, making coherent thought impossible, until, just as quickly, he discovered the humor in Tony's comeback. "Tony the tough guy—no one will believe it," he murmured. Chucky wondered if Tony had just become an asshole like everyone else, or if it was just what he had to do—the best he could do—in the living hell of Pelican Bay.

Somehow Tony, even in defiance, found a way to soften Chucky's heart. Chucky both loved and hated Tony for this, but still he must remain strong. The danger was real, and Tony had been stupid. Tony needed to know there was a price to be paid for defying him. "You're fucked, Tony. You're so fucked up, dog—you'll never make it out of here, not with no help from me, dog." With that, Chucky rolled over to face the wall, letting Tony know they were done.

Chucky's abruptness was fine with Tony, as he had nothing to say. He had done what he had to do, and he knew the risk. Maybe Chucky meant what he had said, maybe he didn't. Maybe he would get over it; maybe Tony would die at Chucky's hand. But no matter what, Tony would have no regrets.

CHAPTER 8

Tribal Warfare

AFTER THE BETRAYAL, things remained tense between Chucky and Tony. They continued to live in peace, occasionally sharing small talk, but mostly they kept to themselves. Solitude wasn't hard for Tony, it being his nature. Chucky, on the other hand, hated it, but he had to convince Tony "the plan" was dead. Silence would do the trick.

Then one night at lockdown, Chucky was nowhere to be found. This meant one of two things: either he'd been shanked bad enough for the infirmary, or he was in the SHU. At first, Tony feared for Chucky, but after reflection he knew Chucky was in the SHU. Chucky had hurt someone.

On the yard the next day, Tony gathered information on what went down. Racial tensions had been heating up. Tony heard a fight had broken out between the white and black inmates in another cellblock, and the black prisoners had badly beaten the whites. This was no surprise, as the white guys were always outnumbered.

Word was the big homies felt the blacks were getting too cocky. Then, something went down between an EME soldier and a BGF. The two were working on the yard when heated words were exchanged. Each side backed their man as the fighting escalated to riot proportions. Responding quickly, the guards broke it up before anyone got seriously hurt.

After closing it down, the men who started it were taken to the SHU. Everything looked good until, after only three days, the BGF inmate was released, while the EME prisoner remained in the SHU. This was a miscarriage of justice in the mind of the Mexican Mafia, as it tipped the balance of power on the yard ever so slightly in favor of the blacks. So, the EME made it known to BGF they needed to keep their man off the yard. The blacks ignored this ultimatum and backed their man up the next day, an act of disrespect the EME shot callers couldn't let go. Only one option remained.

Word went out that war would be going down on the blacks and all the Sureños had to fight. A date, time and place were set. Then the night before, the guards deployed a massive sweep, searching the cells of all Sureños. The prison went into lockdown as inmates caught with weapons were disciplined. It was obvious what had happened: the EME attack had been snitched off. The homeboys were punished, and their weapons confiscated. A contract went out on the likely rat selected by the EME shot callers.

Then Chucky got involved. An EME soldier shanked the snitch on the yard, and he was taken to the infirmary. That wasn't enough for this traitor; a "green light" remained lit on the guy. The big homies told Chucky he needed to come up sick, go to the infirmary and hit the rat again. So, after lying around in bed for a while, Chucky was able to get to the man and drive a plastic shank deep into his shoulder, just below the neck. The hit was to have been in the neck with a bone crusher, leaving the man paralyzed. EME seethed with anger as they had missed the rat twice, and now he would be moved to protective custody where they couldn't get to him.

Chucky went right to the SHU. He would be in isolation for months. Tony's friend was gone; worse, he would get a new cellmate. Tony felt desolate, but he couldn't give in to such an emotion. If he were to survive, he must destroy the last vestiges of his character that could be perceived as weakness. Tony did what he had to do.

Before long, a new cellmate appeared at Tony's door. Pelican Bay always seemed to get two new prisoners for every one they released.[55]

The new prisoner was Mexican, of course, and younger than Tony. Tony treated him with quiet respect, hoping for the same in return. Now was not the time to trust anybody. Pelican Bay had been uglier than usual, and it was sure to get uglier still.

The prison-wide lockdown lasted only three days. Tony hoped that since the guards knew what was up, they would keep it under control. However, it wasn't long before he heard the riot was back on. The EME shot callers had been disrespected, so only one option remained. The word came down that it was on for the next morning and all Sureños would fight.

Wednesday, February 23, 2000, started with the usual rain making the blacktop on the yard shiny. The sky was gray, the air cold at 9:30 a.m. when the men entered the yard.

Inmates arrived in small groups and then waited for sufficient members of their own kind before moving onto their turf. Usually, they remained there until the session was over and then lined up again before walking back to the cellblock. Today, however, some of the Mexican prisoners lingered, while others walked quickly to their turf, searched for a moment, and then returned to the homies hanging out near the center of the yard.

The last of the black inmates were passing through the metal detectors when the battle cry of "Sureños" went up, and the riot was on. The chant of "Sureños" reverberated throughout the yard as the first wave of Mexican prisoners ran at the center of the black lines. Out of nowhere, it seemed, each of the attackers produced a shank. The blacks, caught by surprise, showed good discipline as they formed a perimeter to protect each others' backs. Outnumbered and short on weapons, not one of them turned to run.

The black inmates closest to the invading Sureños were the first to go down. Rather than leave the wounded and move on, the attackers surrounded their victims, striking them over and over again with their weapons or kicking them as they lay on the ground, looking for blood or the sound of crunching bones.

Sureños soon broke through the circles formed by the blacks. They now split smaller groups of black inmates away from the larger whole, surrounded them, and attacked from behind. The blacks fought on valiantly. Their discipline held; no one turned to run. They fought back as best they could, often going bare-fisted against a shank.

All of this did not go unnoticed by the guards, of course. Unfortunately, like the Black inmates, they had been caught by surprise. Once it started, a "stand down" order boomed over the prison loudspeakers. When the inmates ignored the order, a siren sounded, letting the entire prison know that a riot was underway. The guards on the yard quickly came together and determined they were not the intended victims. Getting into formation, they first made an attempt to separate the combatants using pepper spray. But the sheer number of combatants overwhelmed the guards.

Despite their best efforts, the riot continued to grow as more men were drawn into the fight. The guards now implemented a policy of progressive force. A large metal door opened, and a platoon ran into the fight. Decked out in full riot gear, each man advanced in a "V" formation. Breaking through combatants on both sides, prisoners scattered in all directions. But their tactics had little impact, as the battlefield was far too large for localized tactics.

At the fringes, with their backs to the wall, some inmates found temporary refuge, particularly the white prisoners who were neither the victims nor the perpetrators of the assault. The whites remained close to one another, watching with detached amusement. Tony remained on this fringe. Unfortunately, as the riot raged, more and more prisoners were forced into action, either by their peers or attackers on the other side.

The center assault by the guards failed to strike a decisive blow as the number of combatants continued to grow. The guards in the towers, after firing an initial volley of tear gas, had for a time been reduced to spectators. The gas lingered, but the men below continued to savage one another, so a decision to increase the level of force was made. Specially designed rifles, firing rubber and wooden bullets, were issued to the marksmen. Used only in the most dangerous circumstances, the rifles were not supposed to be life threatening, though shots to the face and head could cause permanent damage, such as blindness.

With the order, a new volley of gunfire exploded onto the yard. Prisoners were seen falling to the ground as the rounds fired found men to absorb their impact. But not all the bullets found their mark. Those that missed ricocheted until finding a soft target to land upon.

Still, they did not stop. They fought on and on. Men surrounded by other men smashed their crude weapons into one another until someone faltered. This scene was being repeated throughout the yard. Men everywhere were lying on the ground, usually surrounded by other men beating them, while others, if they kept perfectly still, might at last be left alone as their attackers turned to other prey.

As the fighting continued and the casualties grew, the final option had to be considered. Only one higher level of force remained. Nothing else had worked, and men were dying in the yard below, so the order to use deadly force was made. The marksmen in the towers pulled out Ruger M-14 rifles. A final command blared over the loudspeakers warning the men to "stand down" or "be shot with live ammunition." The order was ignored; the fighting continued.

Meanwhile, Tony had moved safely against the wall at the back of the Mexican lines to avoid involvement. He looked on with amazement at the carnage playing out in front of him. He had seen inmates stabbed before, but he had never seen or imagined anything like this.

Once again, shots exploded from above as the guards hunted the prisoners below. Each shot echoed off the prison walls, and each bullet that missed its mark ricocheted until it found something soft enough to penetrate. Then, Tony heard something that sickened him. It was vaguely familiar; he had heard it before, but he couldn't remember when. Then it came back to him—it was the sound of a bullet exploding through a man's skull.

Up ahead to his right, a young homie he knew only as Miguel collapsed to the ground. Once again, Tony watched as blood and brain matter drained out of a man's head onto the concrete below. Tony dropped to the ground, covering his own head with his hands. Other men went to the ground, as the gunfire above them intensified. Most went by choice, but others were brought down by bullets coming from above.

Tony then heard a faint voice to his left, pleading, "Help me, homie, help me." Tony turned on his stomach in the direction of the voice. He could not tell who had spoken, but when he heard "Help me, homie, help me" again, he knew. It was "Sad Boy," a homeboy about his age, christened Pedro Clark. Pedro was a good-natured homie, so much so that Tony had wondered if his moniker wasn't just a joke. To Pedro, it was no joke; Pedro looked every bit the "Sad Boy." Pedro, on his back, with his legs spread, revealed a gunshot wound to the upper thigh of his left leg, which was bleeding profusely.

Catching only Tony's eyes, Pedro once again begged, "Help me, homie, help me." Tony never hesitated. Crawling on his stomach as trained in the army, he made his way to Pedro. A large pool of blood had collected beneath his leg. Two holes, a round, smaller one on the inside of his thigh and a large gaping hole on the outside, gushed forth fresh blood. Without hesitation, Tony rolled over and sat up. From there, he saw that only a few men were still standing. Tony grabbed the back of his white cotton T-shirt and pulled it off over his head. He then lifted it to his mouth. Tearing a section open at the base, he tore off two long strips. With one strip in each hand, he tied the two together and slipped the pieces beneath Pedro's bleeding thigh just above the bullet holes, pulling the cotton strips together in a knot. With the tourniquet completed, Tony leaned back to see if it worked. The bleeding continued, but not with the same vigor. The openings now seemed to only ooze red instead of pumping it out.

Pedro, who had stoically endured the procedure, now sat up enough to see how it looked. After viewing his condition, he turned to Tony, smiled slightly, saying, "Not bad, homie—not bad at all."

Having finished his work, Tony's attention went back to the battlefield. Through the lingering mist of spent gunpowder and tear gas, he could see that almost everyone, except Pedro and himself, was lying flat on the ground. But for the moans of the wounded, the yard was quiet. The rain of fire from above had finally ended.

A new order blasted from the loudspeakers: "Everyone stay down. Don't move."

For a moment, stillness prevailed. The former sounds of battle had echoed out beyond the prison walls as a silence born of terror prevailed throughout the yard.

Then, in the distance a proud and angry voice rose up, "Sureñooos!" Silence prevailed again for a moment until "Sureñooos" broke out from another corner and then another, and another, slowly growing into a chorus chanted with new conviction throughout the yard. As their courage grew in solidarity, the men of Sureños stood and slowly made their way toward one another, clapping in unison as they regrouped at the center of the yard. Then it was on again. Stoked with the freedom that only defiance can bring, the riot roared anew.

From his vantage point near the wall, Tony could see it all. He wondered how it was that these men were so brave in pursuit of such an evil end. "Why were they willing to kill, and be killed, for nothing more than their hatred of another race?" Then, he realized that wasn't it at all. Hate didn't drive these men. Hate and anger played their roles, but that wasn't what it was about. No, the answer was the same it always had been; it was about respect. Even their fellow inmates had failed to respect them, so what were they to do? Just let it go? No, they had to fight; they had to demand their respect. With respect, they were still alive, but without it, they were already dead. Respect—it was always about respect.

Once again, the guards were taken by surprise. The ultimate solution hadn't worked. Lethal force had been the response, but death had not deterred them. Confusion gripped the guards as the fighting escalated. Precious time passed, but there were no new options, just more "shoot to kill." More force; more death. The order was given to take up firing positions, and again the prisoners were warned to "stand down, or you will be fired upon."

The guards remaining on the yard had largely been able to avoid the conflict. Now with live ammunition bouncing off the walls, some of the inmates turned their anger toward them. Outnumbered and having lost control, fear grew within their ranks. Then, fulfilling their worst fears, a prisoner started running toward them from the center of the yard. Behind him, three other men followed in close pursuit. It was impossible to tell if they were mounting an attack, or if it was just one prisoner running from his attackers. It didn't matter; the guards couldn't take any chances. A modified shotgun leveled at the man in front. Boom! The man's chest imploded. The force of the blast lifted him into the air, propelling him back to land at the feet of the men running after him. There they stopped, turned, and ran back into the battle.

Then, it all happened again. Bullets rained down in torrents from the rifles above. The men below were felled as if they were blades of grass caught beneath a lawn mower. Most went on their own, but others were driven there by impacts from above.

It went on and on, though no man remained standing. Tony, hearing a thump to his right, turned to see a man who had been lying on his side convulse before rolling over on his back, revealing a patch of red running down his neck. The rifle explosions now competed with their echoes as bullets missing their mark struck with fire against the hardened concrete. The moans of the wounded mixed with the screams of the terrified, as men ready to die just a moment ago now begged for mercy—the same mercy they had refused to grant their enemies just a moment ago.

The end came slowly, almost imperceptibly, as the echoes of rifle shots bounced off the prison walls like a box canyon in an old Western, before finally fading into the distance. At last, silence, blessed silence; it was over. Nothing moved below and the only sound was the moaning of the wounded, unable to stifle their pain.

The stillness remained unbroken until the order to stand down boomed from above. This time no one moved, and no one spoke. Then came something new: "Remain where you are. Stretchers will be brought out for the injured." Across the yard, Tony saw a door open, and out ran several teams of stretcher-bearers. They ran first to the severely injured closest to the door. At the far end across the yard, Tony knew it would be a long time before they would get to Pedro and himself. Tony noticed that Pedro's pant leg was soaked with blood and his eyelids hovered half shut. Tony feared his homeboy wouldn't make it.

Pedro then rallied. "I need a smoke, homie. I gotta have a cigarette." Tony considered, then chose not to respond. "I mean it, dog, I gotta smoke. They're here, in my back pocket, homie, help me out."

Tony, amused, smiled softly. Pedro responded indignantly, "What's so funny, dog, you think I'm full of shit or what? I just want a cigarette, alright, man?"

Tony smiled again, saying, "Alright, man."

Pedro, pleased, said, "So get over here, they're in my left back pocket, so when I lean up, you reach under and get them out. You got it, dog?"

Tony nodded, as Pedro tried to push himself up. As soon as Pedro left the ground, he screamed in pain, dropping back down. When he did, Tony noticed Pedro's eyes rolled back up into his head.

"Oh fuck me, man, I'm so fucked up," Pedro cried in obvious agony. "I don't care though. Man, I gotta have a cigarette... you know what I mean?" Once again, Tony nodded in affirmation. "So this time, I'm just going to try and roll over on my right side, man, and you're gonna probably have to help, you know, push me up, and I don't care if I cry like a little baby, man, you gotta help me get up. You understand me, homeboy?" Tony again nodded as Pedro mustered his remaining strength and rolled to his right. Tony reached over with his left hand, pushing Pedro just enough for him to roll all the way over. As his left leg moved over the top of his right, Pedro let out a muffled scream.

"Come on, homie, get them out, the matches too," Pedro demanded through clenched teeth. Tony reached into Pedro's back pocket, retrieved both the box of cigarettes and the matches and then tried to give them to Pedro.

"No, you're gonna have to get it going for me, I don't think I can light it myself," Pedro sniveled. Tony hesitated, realizing that lighting a cigarette right now wasn't a good idea. Pedro noticed Tony's reluctance and pleaded, "Oh come on, man, no one's gonna see you, we're too far away." This didn't persuade Tony; he knew the guards were watching, and at the first sign of trouble they wouldn't hesitate to shoot and worry about the consequences later.

"Look homie, I gotta have a cigarette, I ain't gonna die right here and leave this rat hole without no dignity, man. I'm gonna smoke a cigarette and die like the fucking Marlboro Man, you know what I mean. Are you down with me on this dog, or what?"

Tony let go another, bigger smile, but fought back the impulse to laugh. Opening the box of Marlboros, he took one out, put it between his lips, and struck a match. Once he got it going, he took it from his own lips, reached over and put the filter between Pedro's.

"Thanks, homie, thanks a lot. I told you everything would be alright," and with that, Pedro rolled over onto his back, letting go only a short cry as his wounded leg hit the pavement. Tony wondered if Pedro had just sucked it up better this time, or more likely, if he had lost consciousness.

The cigarette no longer a distraction, Tony looked for the stretchers. The two had been lying there for perhaps ten minutes, but it seemed a lifetime. The guards were systematically removing the wounded while other prisoners were shackled and taken to their cells to be locked down.

Tony and Pedro passed another ten minutes together in silence. Pedro had what he wanted, as all his remaining strength went into smoking the cigarette down to the filter. Tony watched as the smoke mixed with the air, still touched with the sting of tear gas. He took comfort each time the cigarette glowed red, knowing Pedro was still with him. At last, three guards made their way over to them. Two of the guards lifted Pedro roughly onto the stretcher. Pedro let out a slight groan as the spent cigarette fell from his lips. The third guard ordered Tony to "stand and assume the position." Tony complied by getting to his feet, putting his hands behind his back, and spreading his legs. Once handcuffed and shackled, Tony marched across the yard and back into the cellblock. Upon arriving in his cell, the handcuffs and shackles were removed, and he was pushed inside. The metal door slammed closed behind him. It would not open again for three days.

After the riot, Pelican Bay remained in a permanent state of lockdown. After three days, prisoners were allowed out of their cells for only an hour and a half out of each twenty-four, receiving a short period of individual recreation and a shower. Then, they went back to the cells.

The effect of long-term confinement can be devastating. Tony handled it better than most. Since he was never much of a talker, the quiet and the lack of activity didn't seem to bother him. He spent his time reading, writing and working out, maintaining the same rigid schedule, day in and day out.

Lockdown even had some advantages. For instance, Tony no longer had to worry about being assaulted every time he left his cell. The only regular contact he had was with his cellmate. They were getting along tolerably well, though Tony didn't trust him. Trust was for fools. Tony wouldn't be that stupid again.

Tony did find himself missing Chucky, though. No matter what Chucky was, he was never boring. But even that relationship had lost its magic. This Chucky made clear the one time their paths happened to cross.

Chucky had finally made it out of the SHU, and one day his recreation time happened to be the same as Tony's, but he was on another yard. They both managed to make their way to the chain link fence separating them. After getting past hello and talking briefly, Tony decided to torture himself one last time by asking Chucky about the plan. Chucky got indignant, calling Tony "a fool" for mentioning it. Tony tried to apologize, but Chucky would have none of it. Turning his back on Tony, Chucky stomped away, muttering, "You fucked it all up dog, not me." That was the last Tony saw of Chucky at Pelican Bay.

A few months later, Tony heard that Chucky had transferred to another prison, but no one seemed to know where. Even if Tony had wanted to write Chucky, he didn't know where to mail it.

Tony ran into Pedro Clark a few times after the riot. It took Pedro a while to get out of the infirmary. They had done emergency surgery to repair the femoral artery in his left thigh. The first time Pedro saw Tony, he showed him the scars on either side of his thigh and told Tony that the doctor had said, "That man probably saved your life." From then on, Pedro would always thank his homeboy for the cigarette whenever they met.

With the loss of Chucky and his lack of contact with other prisoners, Tony began retreating further and further into himself. It was safer there, if not entirely sane. He began living more within the confines of his own mind.

Day after day, week after week, and then month after month, Tony withdrew further into himself. Darkness reigned over his life. He had been a fool. The hope that he once had was a delusion. As Chucky made clear, hope was for weaklings unable to face reality. Tony would survive, and survive without hope. Hope in Pelican Bay was cruel. To believe in it was evil. It took a man's strength and left him vulnerable. Tony was finally convinced that it was better to live without hope than die like a fool.

CHAPTER 9

Commitment

LEN WAS CRUSADING again. He had been my regular
investigator for years now, and he was good, oh so very good at
his job. In fact, he was so good he made me look good, and for
that I was willing to put up with a lot, but this was getting ridiculous.
I had told him no at least five times on this one: no more crusades;
no more battles against the government on behalf of some poor,
misunderstood, possibly innocent (yeah, right), gang banger being
railroaded by law enforcement, who, ah, by the way has no money! I
had been in private practice for more than fifteen years, and I was tired
of beating my head against the wall for nothing. I had mouths to feed,
three other lawyers, two secretaries and, oh yeah, a private investigator
who always got paid. No more pro bono, not me, not now anyway—
there were too many unpaid bills and not enough paying clients to
justify another crusade.

Len knew just how to get to me, he always did. Len had my respect,
which was not easy to come by. What I admired wasn't just how good
he was at his job, but where he had come from and how he had done it.
Leonard Newcomb had grown up in Oxnard without a father and not
much of a mother. His mother was the black sheep of a well-respected
New England family who no longer tolerated her rebellious behavior.

Men would come and go out of Len's home, some good, and some not so good. As he became a teenager, Len grew tall and strong and was quickly recognized by his high school football coach. Through football, he found the discipline and camaraderie that would act as a foundation for his life. More importantly, Len began attending a youth group at a local church. The kids he met there and values he adopted kept Len out of trouble and on the right side of the law. When Len graduated in 1968 from Oxnard High School, he was named one of the City of Oxnard's outstanding young citizens.

After a short stint in the Navy as a medic, Len returned to Oxnard and enrolled in the Police Academy. For more than twenty years, Len was an "Oxnard Cowboy," first as a patrol officer and then as a detective. Len was true blue law enforcement, totally dedicated to the principles for which they stood. In 1981, he was named one of the "Policemen of the Year," and later he was elected President of the Oxnard Police Officers' Association. Len received the highest honor bestowed in his local community when he was given the prestigious "Medal of Valor" by the City of Oxnard for saving the life of a man who almost drowned in a boating accident off a local beach.

Len's career in law enforcement seemed set until a tragic event altered it forever. On December 2, 1993, he was working with his friend Jim "O.B." O'Brian at the Oxnard station when a call came in about a gunman walking into the local Employment Development Department and shooting everyone in sight. There were reportedly seven fatalities at the scene, and the perpetrator had escaped. Len and O.B. scrambled out of the station in separate cars in hot pursuit. The suspect ran into a barricade set up by police and, when stopped, he turned to shoot at his pursuers. The shooting stopped as the suspect jumped out of his car and began fleeing on foot. Len stayed right behind him until it was clear where they were headed.

As they reached the Employment Development Department in the neighboring City of Ventura, the man turned on him to fire, but Len shot first, hitting him several times. As he approached the man bleeding to death on the ground, Len felt a sense of rage and exhilaration that he would never forget. When he returned to his car and saw what had happened at the barricade, he found more cause for rage. The shooter had shot a hole through the front window of O.B.'s car. O.B. had taken a bullet in the head and died from his wounds at the scene. Devastated, Len had gotten the bad guy, but failed to save his friend.[56]

Len continued to work at Oxnard P.D., though things would never be the same. Before long, conflicts with his supervisors increased. He found more and more things wrong with Oxnard P.D., and they in turn had problems with Len. Finally, in one fit of anger, Len referred to his commander's wife as "a bitch" and received a formal letter of reprimand. Incensed, Len barged into his supervisor's office and declared, "I am never going to kill anyone again!"

The police psychologist paid Len a visit and diagnosed him with post-traumatic stress, placing him on involuntary leave. After a prolonged legal battle, for which he still harbors some resentment, Len was retired from Oxnard P.D.

Feeling betrayed and disillusioned, Len began putting on weight. He had some issues to work through. His career in law enforcement over, he now realized not all of his brothers in blue had the missionary zeal that had guided him through his career. Looking in from the outside, he didn't like what he saw coming out of Oxnard P.D. Consequently, Len gathered his courage and made a bold decision. With the support of a loving wife and family, Len went into business for himself and became a defense investigator.

Most of Len's former colleagues were shocked, and some were downright hostile. The animosity only served to motivate him to prove them wrong. Whenever Len took on a new defense case, he did it with something to prove. This was what I loved most about Len; he truly believed in what he was doing. He had seen and done it all, and now he was on our side.

Despite my respect for Len, I really didn't want to hear any more about some Colonia homeboy who had gunshot residue all over his hands, but really wasn't the shooter in a homicide up in Santa Barbara. Len eventually stopped telling me that this would be the "biggest case to hit this area in years" and that this guy, Tony Estrada, had fallen victim to a total miscarriage of justice that sent him to prison for life.

This time, however, Len had a different approach, a totally unfair one, but one he knew would work. He appealed to my ego.

"So, we have this hearing coming up because the judge wants to review the evidence and see if he wants to grant Estrada a new trial, or whatever. So I need to know, say hypothetically, Phil, what would you have me do if you were the lawyer on this case?"

I knew what Len was doing, suckering me in, but he was doing it so well.

"Well, you know what we would do, we would subpoena everybody, and all the records, and we wouldn't start until we got them all."

There, I had said it, and now the hook.

"Damn it, I knew it! I knew that's what you'd say, but I am telling you, Phil, this clown won't let me subpoena anybody!"

"Oh that's garbage, Len, how can a lawyer have a hearing in a murder case and not subpoena anyone or anything?" Recovering now, I was not about to get sucked in without a fight.

"I'm telling you, Phil, I keep asking him if I can just subpoena even law enforcement in Ventura, and he won't let me do it. He says it's all in the Writ, he doesn't need any witnesses, just the tape, and some witness declarations."

Something Len said got my attention. "What law enforcement in Ventura?"

Len was coy now, about to set the hook. "Just Haney, McMaster and maybe a few others," he said coolly.

"You mean to tell me Bill Haney and Dennis McMaster are testifying for the defense?"

I had bitten down hard. I had known Bill Haney for years. I was a veteran defense lawyer when Haney started right out of law school at the Ventura D.A.'s office. I watched as he became an instant success, a golden boy who rose through the ranks of the office with lightning speed. Most recently, he was assigned to gang prosecutions where he had hooked up with Detective Dennis McMaster of the Oxnard P.D.

Haney intrigued me, but the thought of Dennis McMaster testifying for the defense shocked my soul. I knew Detective McMaster well. When I started as a deputy public defender almost twenty years ago, McMaster already had been a street cop in Oxnard for a couple years. Being young and filled with righteous indignation, it wasn't long before I came up against McMaster and took a few shots at him.

Half the police reports coming into the office out of Oxnard seemed to have McMaster as the arresting officer. McMaster hovered over Oxnard like some kind of superhero lawman—pulling people over on the slimmest of hunches, breaking down doors, falling out of trees. Somehow he always came up with an airtight legal explanation to justify his tactics. Like everyone else in the public defender's office, the only recourse I had against McMaster's tactics was setting his cases for suppression motions. One time, and one time only, early on, I caught him on a fairly obscure issue and got my client's case dismissed.

That dismissal remained my only victory, as McMaster pretty much ran the board on me from then on. After that, every time I had a motion with him I noticed he carried photocopies of the case law and huddled with his prosecutor before testifying. Then, the prosecutor would pull out McMaster's research and argue by quoting the portions he had highlighted. Invariably, McMaster found a precedent that provided him with sufficient cause for his arrest. This was the McMaster I knew.

With this in mind, I couldn't see how McMaster would ever testify for the defense. He would never concede anyone in law enforcement had done something wrong. No way—McMaster, the number one law enforcement terminator, wasn't about to be re-programmed. Something definitely was up.

Len had let my last question linger, knowing it was rhetorical. So after letting it sink in, he went on, "Sure, they've got to testify, they have to lay the foundation for the wire. That's what I'm upset about."

"The wire," I thought. I knew better than to ask, but I couldn't help myself. "What's the wire, Lenny?"

"Oh, I haven't told you about the wire yet?" Len smirked. "The wire, the tape recording they made in jail, this is the best part. They got this gang banger, some big homie down in the Colonia, to admit he was dirty, a real bad boy. Dennis could never make a case on him. No one would ever testify against him."

McMaster had been one of Len's Police Explorer Scouts, so their friendship went way back. Len still had some friends in law enforcement, and Dennis McMaster was one of them.

I didn't want to look stupid, but I still didn't quite get it, "Why are you calling it a wire if he confessed on tape, Len?"

Len looked smug. "Because there was a snitch, of course. They had to wire him up and put him in with this Colonia gangbanger. You should hear this tape, Phil, it's something else."

A snitch in a Colonia Chiques case was a new one on me. Colonia had a twisted but rigidly enforced code of honor that I had never seen broken. My familiarity came from having represented more than my share of the homeboys from Oxnard, and I had to admit I respected some of their ethics. Wires and snitching on some big homie in Colonia intrigued me, as Len knew it would.

"So, who's the snitch, Len? How did they get a homie to rat off one of his partners? What did they do, give him a misdemeanor on a life sentence?"

"No, that's not it, really. This guy has already done most of his time, at Pelican Bay no less, and he's still in prison, so he didn't get much of a deal."

"I guess not," I said. "So who is this guy, Len, anybody we know?"

"No, I don't think so, he's been away for a while. I can't even remember his real name, but his moniker is pretty good; they call him 'Chucky,' you know, after the Chucky doll. Guess he's been around the blocks a few times, gotten all shot up more than once, and lived to fight again, so that's why they call him 'Chucky.'" Len was smiling now.

"Sounds like a standup guy, but it doesn't make sense, Len. Why would a guy like that roll over for nothing? He could've done his time sitting on his head."

"Because Estrada didn't do it, Phil, that's what I keep telling you. The guy's innocent, and Chucky was his cellie, and the two of them thought this thing up in Pelican, and now here they are, made it all the way back on a Writ."

"This is too good to be true," I thought. "Something's got to be missing here." I hit back with, "So if this kid didn't do the shooting, then why in the world did he have gun residue all over his hands?"

"Mere circumstantial evidence, my friend, subject to two reasonable interpretations, as the GSR expert will testify. One is he shot a gun, of course; the other he was in 'an environment where gunshot residue was present.'[57] In other words, he was in the garage when the shooting went down, but he didn't pull the trigger." Len finished his argument with a look of triumph. Like a fish on a line, I was hooked and patiently reeled in. But hooking me wasn't good enough; he had the gaff in reserve.

"You know, Phil, instead of you asking all these legal questions, why don't you just take a look at the reports yourself? In fact, you can just have this copy here." With that, Len slid a three-ring binder about three inches thick across my desk.

"Something to do in my spare time, Len?" I jibed as the gaff sliced my side. I had expected an answer, but Len just grinned. So, I countered, "What are you going to use for reports while I look at these?"

"Oh I have my copy down in the car," Len said as he slid the filet knife up my soft underbelly. Squirming and gasping my last breath of freedom, I gurgled one final defense I was sure he hadn't considered.

"You got permission from the client's attorney to give me all this, of course, didn't you, Lenny?"

Len hesitated, looked disappointed for a moment, and then smiled larger than ever.

"No, I didn't get his permission, but I don't work for him. I was hired by the family; he's too cheap to pay me himself. No, I got the client's permission."

Landed and packed in ice, I thought, but said nothing. Len knew me well, cautious to a fault; I always made sure we never did anything that could be used against us later. In our business, ethical dilemmas and potential dangers lurked in every corner, making the first rule: never create any of your own. Len, more inclined to charge ahead, operated as if each new battle was our last. This time he had covered all the bases, and he knew it.

"I gotta get going," Len said as he stood. "But there's one more thing you might want to know. The client, Tony Estrada, his mother tells me that he became a Christian in prison." Len turned and walked out, leaving the thick binder behind.

"Len really wanted this one," I thought. He had not only hooked me and reeled me into the boat, but now he had smacked me upside the head to make sure I didn't get out. He knew my weak spots and was willing to exploit them. I had been raised by a mother who regularly quoted scripture calling for the care of "the poor, the widowed, and the orphaned." It wasn't until I became a criminal defense attorney that I took my mother's teaching seriously. It was the only way I could make sense of it all. To me, when the job was broken down to its most basic elements, it was Good vs. Evil, just that simple—a continuing fight for supremacy fought over one soul at a time.

I was aware that my philosophy toward the work was unconventional, to say the least. It didn't bother me; I had been at it long enough to know I couldn't do the job and be concerned about what other people thought. Over time, I quit trying to explain how I could represent people when I knew they were guilty. No explanation ever sufficed.

Eventually, I realized my job offered tremendous freedom—freedom from anyone else's expectations. As long as the client knew I was with him, I could define victory on my own terms. If my way included a little faith on the side, so be it.

Thus began my commitment to Tony Estrada. Over the next couple of weeks, whenever there was a break in the action, or at night after court, I plowed through the reports with a passion. What I read first was like nothing I had ever seen. The most recent reports and memos had all been prepared by Dennis McMaster, Bill Haney or the DA investigator working for Haney. It was perfectly organized, and everything in the investigation had been memorialized. More impressive was what they'd done and how they had done it.

Sometime in June of 1999, Marta Diego, Tony Estrada's aunt, talked to McMaster. She and her sister Angela Rodriguez went to McMaster as a last resort, after trying several other detectives first. Since McMaster had testified against Estrada in his trial, they didn't trust him. However, since no one else would listen, they finally approached McMaster, and, to their surprise, he was interested.

They brought him a message from an inmate at Pelican Bay he had arrested on a home invasion robbery. Chucky knew McMaster had a street sense of honor.

Despite the fact McMaster had sent Chucky away for twelve years, there still existed a certain respect between the men. McMaster knew Chucky had given him a real bad boy in the past: the shooter in several drive-by shootings. Innocent victims, or "civilians" as Chucky called them, were getting hurt. Chucky knew the shooter was out of control, so he went to McMaster, taking a sociopath off the streets.

In the message to McMaster, Chucky made subtle reference to his prior good deed and his desire to help again. McMaster, ever ready to follow up a lead, made arrangements to take a trip to Pelican Bay.

McMaster's reception at Pelican Bay was anything but pleasant. Navigating a visitor through all the hi-tech security was an imposition on the guards. McMaster felt like an outsider invading a forgotten world no one cared about, filled with forgotten men no one should ever visit. Just finding a place to meet away from other inmates was a challenge.

When Chucky was finally brought into the small office, he was shackled hand and foot. Thinking they might be a while, McMaster asked the guard to remove Chucky's cuffs, a request with which the officer reluctantly complied. When finally left alone, Chucky got right to his feet, pacing the short space of the office. McMaster, all business all the time, started with "Well, whatta 'ya got?" "Shhh," Chucky scolded, pointing to the ceiling, "We don't trust nobody in here." Looking down on the small note pad and pencil on the desk, Chucky said, "We do this all in writing, and leave nothing behind."

"How's that possible?"

"You write your question, I'll show you." McMaster, still sitting, put pen to paper, repeating his initial question. Chucky took the pad, read, tore out the paper, again tore away the portion unwritten upon, tore the note into small pieces, then put the pieces in his mouth and started to chew. With a swallow, Chucky grabbed for pen and paper and wrote a much smaller note in reply, turned it around for McMaster to read, and upon seeing him nod, Chucky again tore the note into small pieces and destroyed the evidence by eating it.

McMaster, having some compassion, and not wanting to waste any more paper, wrote a small "Why?"

"Can't trust guards" was Chucky's next swallow.

"Who?"

"Capper."

"When?"

"Lot 10 shooting in S.B."

"How?"

"38, 5 shots."

As Chucky chewed, McMaster bought in, "a .38 caliber revolver, I'll bet, Capper's weapon of choice."

"Who?"

"Tony cellie."

This revelation caught McMaster as he calculated the odds of the two homeboys from Oxnard winding up in the same prison, let alone cellmates. "You in?"

"All the way."

"Why?"

"It's not right, letting his primo do his time."

Looking Chucky straight in the eye, McMaster knew it was true. He knew it back then, and he knew it for sure now. His theory of gang shootings was once again affirmed. Most homeboys will go along for the ride, but only the truly malevolent will pull the trigger. Capper was a shooter; he shot those boys in that parking garage.

McMaster's Holmesian pride quickly faded as he contemplated his own complicity. "I helped them convict that kid, and I knew better. Capper's out terrorizing the streets, and some kid just out of the army, with no record, is doing forty-one to life in Pelican Bay, dear God." The magnitude of this revelation shook McMaster to his law enforcement core. No longer was he the good guy, the cowboy wearing the white hat, the protector of the innocent. He tried to tell them, but the response was always the same, "We've got our shooter; stay out of our business. Just do your job and testify about the Colonia Chiques. It's not your case."

McMaster complied, and lived to regret it. Regret soon turned into anger and then commitment. "It's not right, that's all there is to it. I can't just go home and sleep every night knowing there's a guy in jail who shouldn't be there."[58]

Replacing rage with reality, McMaster took the pen from Chucky and wrote the hard question, "Wear wire, snitch?" Then, he folded the paper, once again looking Chucky in the eyes with a gravity of purpose that was unmistakable.

Now it was Chucky's turn, his moment of hard truth. That word, the label, "snitch," violated everything he lived and stood for. Slammed down, with the EME on the inside, he "weren't no snitch." His code of honor had been violated. How dare this cowboy from Oxnard even mention the word. What was he thinking?!

But that was just it, he was thinking. No, more than that, he was feeling. Compassion; nothing about the word made sense, but it wouldn't go away. Chucky bit down hard on his lip, and slowly, almost imperceptively, nodded his head slowly up and then down.

McMaster asked nothing more of Chucky, respecting the man in the moment. Nodding once in return, he stood and turned away, heading for the door. As he did, he thought he noticed a small streak of red making its way down Chucky's chin.

CHAPTER 10

Unlikely Rivals

HAVING GOTTEN HIS answer, McMaster left Pelican Bay, making plans for the operation. He knew he would need help from the Ventura D.A.'s office. He turned to his friend, Bill Haney. Haney and McMaster had been working together for some time. Haney was in charge of the gang unit, and McMaster was his best detective working the county's most violent gang, Colonia.

Haney listened to the details of McMaster's investigation and never once doubted its authenticity. When later questioned by a fellow prosecutor as to why he so readily accepted McMaster's theory, Haney explained it simply, "You have to understand, our information source was Detective Dennis McMaster, and he's not your average detective."[59]

When McMaster told him the wrong guy was in prison for a homicide committed in another county, Haney never hesitated. He immediately started a campaign within his office to set up the wire operation. The response from Haney's superiors gave more weight to the sensitive political turf they were treading, so before the operation could be authorized, a concerted effort to bring the Santa Barbara D.A.'s office on board had to be made.

In the early part of July 1999, McMaster contacted Hilary Dozer regarding the sting operation. At first, Dozer appeared interested, listening carefully to the new information.

Not just relying upon Chucky, McMaster interviewed two other witnesses who alleged Capper admitted to the shooting. Rochelle Gomez, cousin to both Tony Estrada and Capper, had now come forward with her husband Mauricio, and she told McMaster that Capper had confessed to them at a Super Bowl party shortly after the homicide. Capper provided them with intimate details of the shooting, including a precise description of the murder weapon. Monica Rodriguez, also at the party, told them how she had tried to discourage her husband from getting involved. When he insisted, she drove their car through the parking lot until she witnessed the shooting and then picked Capper up just outside of Lot 10.

McMaster gave this information to Dozer, but Dozer waited months to respond. McMaster's inquiries were ignored, and when Dozer finally responded he scolded the detective for working a case outside of his jurisdiction. He reminded McMaster they were already aware of Rochelle Gomez' statement, since she had provided a similar declaration to Joe Lax, Tony's original attorney, when he made a motion for a new trial. Dozer informed McMaster that Rochelle Gomez had been questioned early in the investigation and had never provided this information. Since Estrada had been convicted, Dozer was not surprised family members were now coming forward trying to get him out of prison. McMaster refused to be discouraged by Dozer's denials. He continued calling Dozer to discuss the matter, but when Dozer would respond it was with increasing hostility. Finally, after nearly three months of frustration, McMaster gave up on Dozer and reported back to Haney.

Haney began a similar effort, with similar results. Initially receptive to Haney's inquiries, Dozer even expressed a desire to cooperate. However, as time went on Dozer never followed up with an actual commitment. Haney, being the boy scout of prosecutors, could not understand Dozer's tactics. In Haney's mind, Dozer had made a commitment to follow the truth to wherever it might lead. How could he ethically do anything else? They were the good guys, and the good guys love the truth, no matter what the truth might be. The wire operation would either fail to prove Estrada's innocence, thus vindicating Dozer, or set an innocent man free. Dozer's failure to communicate, much less cooperate, at first confused Haney and then angered him. After more than ten months of delay and frustration, Haney finally concluded Dozer had no intention of pursuing the truth. If the operation was to go down, they would do it in spite of Santa Barbara law enforcement, not in cooperation with them.

Haney's next hurdle was convincing his bosses the operation was justified. Persuading them to go out on such a political limb seemed unlikely.

Haney had one trump card, and he was willing to play it for McMaster. Throughout his career, he had maintained a reputation of integrity. Well-liked and respected within his office, Haney had come to symbolize prosecutorial ethics. When issues arose for other prosecutors, Haney was the one they went to for guidance. Haney had researched the law, and it called for the sting operation to go forward.

Finally, in April of 2000, Haney wrote a memo concluding Santa Barbara law enforcement had violated their ethical obligations under *Brady v. Maryland*. He didn't stop there but explained that the Ventura D.A.'s office also had a "free-standing" *Brady* obligation to "discover material exculpatory evidence."[60]

The landmark decision of *Brady v Maryland (1963),* Haney argued, places an affirmative constitutional duty on a prosecutor to disclose evidence of innocence to a defendant. This duty also included police agencies, requiring law enforcement officers to notify the defense of any potential exculpatory information. Normally, this would be done through the local D.A.'s office, but when that agency refuses to comply with the law an independent prosecutorial agency must fulfill the duty. In light of this precedent, Haney concluded his memo by recommending the sting operation go forward without the approval of the Santa Barbara D.A.'s office.

Decisions of this magnitude are not made by lower-level management. The matter made its way through the chief deputy and ultimately to Ventura County's district attorney, Michael Bradbury. Bradbury had been D.A. for more than twenty years, and his reputation as a hard-nosed prosecutor was well established. Recently, he had made it known he would not be running again. His choice as the next D.A. would be his longtime chief deputy and friend, Greg Totten. With the next election right around the corner, a feud between his office and Santa Barbara was not a good political move.

Bradbury could play it safe by simply telling Haney it was not their problem. Instead, Bradbury lived up to his tough reputation and history of unpopular but principled decisions. Bradbury gave Haney the go-ahead and put Totten in charge.

Despite everyone's commitment to the operation, they knew the odds were against them. This was nothing new for Haney and McMaster; few of their gang investigations were ever easy. No matter—their resolve was now unshakeable. They knew something was wrong, terribly wrong, and they were not about to let it go.

CHAPTER 11

The Operation

HANEY'S FIRST ORDER of business was bringing Chucky back from Pelican Bay to the Ventura County Jail. The prison bureaucracy responded slowly, but finally in the early part of May 2000, Chucky transferred to Ventura. The wait for Chucky gave Haney and McMaster time to deal with their biggest problem: how could they get Chucky and Capper together? Not willing to release Chucky onto the streets of Oxnard, Capper would have to meet Chucky in jail. Chucky thought he could coax Capper into visiting him, but he wasn't sure the visitation room would work out. Using the telephone to speak through a thick-windowed partition while deputy sheriffs watch behind smoked glass was not an ideal environment. But there seemed no alternative, so plans were made to do it the hard way.

Then, as providence would have it, the operation caught a huge break. Capper got arrested on charges of attempted murder, assault with a deadly weapon, possession of narcotics for sale, and a gang allegation for street terrorism. Capper and a few of his homeboys had tried to crash a party at a restaurant in Oxnard. When they were told to leave, a fight ensued in which Capper slit a man's throat, piercing his carotid artery. Fortunately, the man eventually recovered, but Capper's troubles had just begun. For good measure, the Ventura D.A. added drug charges to his complaint, which had been part of a long-term narcotics investigation. His bail was set at $780,000, more than even he could afford. Since it looked like Capper would be in for a while, a chance meeting between the two would be easier to arrange.

Still, preparing the operation took longer than expected. In the meantime, Capper and Chucky were in jail together for several months. Occasionally, they ran into each other. When they did, Capper wanted to talk about how they had taken care of Capper's "Tony problem." Chucky's usual response was to scold Capper for talking too loosely. This tactic only caused Capper to trust Chucky more.

Capper and Chucky soon discovered they had a direct pipeline to one another. Chucky's cell was on the floor above Capper's, and the steel plumbing ran down from above, connecting to the cells below. By talking directly into the toilet, inmates could hear one another on various party lines. Capper and Chucky were on just such a line. One night Capper started talking about his Tony problem, but Chucky immediately cut him off, reminding him "others" were listening. In fact, just to prove his point, he told Capper to watch the deputy sheriff in the unit's observation booth. While Capper watched, Chucky screamed obscenities into the toilet. The deputy jumped up, and ripped out an earphone. Capper laughed hysterically and Chucky soon joined him as Capper described the scene back through the pipes.

Chucky did, however, communicate some Tony-related things to Capper. Through a series of short and sometimes confusing messages, Chucky let Capper know a problem had arisen with some big homies back at Pelican Bay. The hit on Tony had never been authorized. Chucky and Capper needed to come up with some "paperwork" justifying the hit. The EME would not tolerate a hit on a little brother who was just trying to help himself out. Some kind of proof that Tony had been trying to snitch on Capper had to materialize, and it needed to be in the form of "paperwork."

"Paperwork" was anything in writing, but particularly any court transcript, document or police report confirming the accusation.[61] Simply calling someone a snitch was not enough. The accuser had to prove it before any retaliation would be ratified. Failure to provide paperwork required that the accuser be disciplined.

Depending on the nature of the accusation, discipline could be as extreme as a full-scale hit. Chucky began pushing Capper to come up with paperwork on Tony. He reminded Capper that he likely would be in prison soon, and when he got there he would need paperwork on Tony, or he would have a problem. The more Chucky pushed Capper for paperwork, the more anxious Capper became. Chucky maneuvered Capper like the master prison manipulator he had become.

Finally, the day of the sting arrived: August 25, 2000. The day before, McMaster and Detective Trent Jewell of the Oxnard Police met with Chucky to plan it out.

Capper had a bail review set for the next day. Chucky and Capper were to be placed in a small holding cell located between two courtrooms. Chucky would be there for an appearance in the courtroom next to the one Capper was to appear in. Both Chucky and the holding cell would have recording equipment.

The hard part would be getting Capper to talk about the events of Lot 10. On this, Chucky rose to new heights of ingenuity. He proposed a fictitious letter to himself from a shot caller at Pelican Bay known as Macho.* Since the letter would have come from a prison to a jail, the guards would have read it. So it had to be written in a kind of code including a mixture of English and Spanish words, often called Spanglish. Much of the letter contained common greetings and references to other inmates they both knew. The true message of the letter was communicated toward the end, like this:

ANYWAYS THE REASON WHY I AM WRITING YOU IS TO LET YOU KNOW YOUR CARNAL ESTRADA DROVE UP PURO PEDO. HE'S TRYING TO MAKE THINGS RIGHT FOR HIMSELF BUT HE HASN'T ORDERED THE NEWSPAPER YET SO WHAT'S UP? THE HOMIE "G" WANTS TO KNOW HOW WE CAN RESOLVE THIS ISSUE CAUSE YOUR CARNAL IS ACTING LIKE A CHIHUAHUA.

---

*   Macho is a pseudonym for an actual inmate at Pelican Bay at the time.

ORALE PUES HOMIE BE COOL AND HOPE TO
SEE YOU SOON. STAY OUT OF TROUBLE, PUTO!
GET BACK AT ME "ASAP" AND TRY TO ORDER
THE HOMIE THE NEWSPAPER LIKE YOU SAID
FOOL. SEND OUR LOVE TO THE CAMARADAS!

CON MUCHO RESPECTO
MACHO[62]

Chucky dictated the letter to Detective Jewell and even suggested a drawing of a cartoon character in the middle. All of this was designed to confuse the "reader" so that only the truly "con wise" could interpret its true meaning. This Chucky would do when he showed Capper the letter. After copies were made to preserve it as evidence, the strategy session concluded.

The next day Chucky was awakened at 6:00 a.m. and fitted with the recording device. He hadn't slept, so the early call for the fitting didn't bother him. McMaster met Chucky in a small room in the jail. Given the letter along with a small piece of plastic, Chucky folded it into a square and wrapped it in the plastic. Then he put the plastic in his mouth, holding it between his cheek and gum.

What happened next is all recorded on tape.[63] It begins with someone wishing Chucky "good luck." Then, Chucky can be heard walking out of the room and down a long underground tunnel connecting the jail to the courthouse. The walk lasts for several minutes, and the clanking of Chucky's leg irons as he moves down the corridor dominates the audio. The occasional guttural sound coming from deep within his scarred esophagus is the only exception to the sound of chains clanking.

Next, he passes through a metal detector and the machine sounds the alarm, but an exception is made as the deputy in charge allows him to proceed. Taken upstairs by elevator to the wired holding cell, he is left there by himself.

Chucky would later describe his fear at this moment as being greater than anything he had ever experienced. Riots and drive-bys and beatings could be written off as the random events in life, things he had no control over. But this move, Chucky had orchestrated himself. Paranoia gripped him as he convinced himself the wires taped to his body could be easily seen. He knew his exposure as a snitch was a certainty. He thought his life was over, and the only thing left was how would it end.

For what seems like a very long time, the recording only picks up the clanking of shackles as Chucky paces back and forth in the cell. Finally, the turn of the lock and opening of the heavy metal door signals the point of no return as Capper walks in. Chucky, fully committed, turns to meet his old friend with a smile.

CHAPTER 12

The Wire

A FTER HEARING THE clank of the steel door closing, Chucky shrieks, "What's up, fool!" to which Capper responds, "What are you doing, fool!"

For a while, the two men chatter about old friends from the neighborhood and what landed them in jail this time. Then, abruptly shifting, Chucky tells Capper he has a letter he must see. Chucky can be heard extracting the letter from his mouth, and there is the faint sound of paper rustling as he unwraps it, and gives it to Capper. A few moments of silence follow as Capper reads it. Concluding with the exclamation, "Man, Puto, that smell," Capper is heard ripping up the letter and then a toilet flushes. At this, Chucky laughs ruefully as he has now maneuvered Capper into a discussion about their Tony problem. Chucky presses Capper for some paperwork he can use to clear their hit on Tony with the shot callers in Pelican Bay. Chucky tells Capper, "... see it won't fall back really on me, but at the same time they gonna scold me if I don't go with no fucking paperwork, homie."*

---
* The language used from here on out is a synopsis of verbatim statements contained in a transcript later admitted as evidence in court.

Capper whines to Chucky that he has no paperwork, but hopes to get some from his former attorney. He then offers that his aunt (Angela Rodriguez) had called him two days after the shooting and discussed what happened. Capper says this is proof that Tony broke the "code of silence" by telling his mother what really happened in Lot 10, "... and so that's how my aunt knew everything."

Capper tells Chucky about how his wife, Monica, has nightmares about Lot 10 and then, in a voice barely above a whisper, "*I did it ... I did it,* and she drove me away." Chucky is coy, feigning disbelief; he says he had always thought "Zap" was the shooter. Capper then tells Chucky about how the police put pressure on him to talk when he was in jail in Santa Barbara. They threatened to arrest his wife unless he talked, but he didn't admit anything. "So why am I gonna tell 'em something?"

Chucky agrees, "You gonna tell on yourself?"

Capper goes on to tell how the detectives' threat to arrest his wife and take his children into foster care was so terrifying that he even considered confessing: "... if worse comes to worse, I'll tell em, ya know, fuck it. I'll do it and just let my wife go."

The conversation drifts away for a while until Chucky subtly brings it back to what led up to the shootings. Capper explains what he told the police about the Hurricane Club, saying,

> "I come back and these fools and Zap are chilling ... they told me they're kicking us out. They kicked us out the front and I don't know what happened to those guys. And then they ... they go, well, how come you guys didn't wanna leave? I go, what are you talking about, leave? I left. Me and my wife left ... We went out to the car. So, and then, um he's telling me, what about the other guys. What happened to them? I go, I don't know what happened. He said, you didn't hear no shots, I said, no, I didn't hear no shots, I was gone man. I left. He goes, 'alright, so that's all I said homie' and then we go to prelim [preliminary hearing] and then my lawyer's telling me that, there's like two vatos saying that I was a peacemaker inside ... ."

Chucky breaks into laughter, and Capper joins him gleefully, saying, "That's why the juras [police] tripped out. You know what I mean," at which they both laugh uproariously.

After the laughter dies down, Chucky artfully moves Capper back to the shooting by asking, "And what happened? These vatos started acting stupid, outside or what?"

"Yeah, they started acting stupid and then outside they took 'em out the back, and they came, they came to where the homies were, but see, I was telling, I was telling ... let's jam, homie, ... "Let's jam. Fuck this bullshit, dog. And so then they started talking and I told him, chale vato [to hell with it]. Fuck it homie, I'm gone, homies... Me and my hyna and his hyna, we're jamming, homie, we said fuck you, we're leaving. But Tony stayed there and he starts yelling dog, he's yelling Capper, Capper, he keeps yelling Capper, Capper, and I'm over here. I'm upstairs, getting in the car, and I'm hearing him. I had to ... dog, I couldn't leave him homie ... No, so I said man I can't leave him there right ... and I grabbed the quete [gun] and I put it like this and I go downstairs...And then I see fuck Mitchell Sanchez ..., I don't know, and he goes Capper, Capper, Capper, he started yelling ... fuck and I seen him, homie. And I just, BAM, BAM ... [fired the gun]"

Chucky asks, "How many?" and Capper responds "four" and then describes how he grabbed Tony in an attempt to get him to leave. Then, he says someone took the gun from him and he watched as the vatos were beaten. Capper explains to Chucky that Tony got caught and convicted because he didn't want to leave and how "... he got gunpowder on him."

Capper justifies the shooting by saying "... *I did it ... I did it for him*," referring to Tony. Capper is now indignant because, as he tells it, he "saved" Tony, and Tony was now snitching him off. So he had to "... tell his own Mom and Dad that he did it, but that he did it for Tony." However, Capper expresses no regrets, as he explains he did it "... instead of leaving him there, where he could've gotten killed."

The conversation shifts as Capper tells Chucky how this might help them. Since Capper "did it," Tony is now snitching him off, which was the needed justification for the hit on Tony. Capper tells Chucky he must take this explanation back to Pelican Bay with him because "... that's what happened, dog."

The conversation drifts away again and settles on the major players at Pelican Bay, and whether they're concerned about Capper. Capper knows some of the inmates and tells Chucky that if they "had a problem" with him, he thinks he would have known it. Shortly after this the tape runs out, and though it cannot be heard, a jailer enters the cell and calls Chucky out for his "court appearance." It is 10:30 a.m.

Chucky is taken to a courtroom, but there is no judge present. McMaster tries to debrief Chucky, but Chucky's excited jabber makes little sense. Finally, he tells them Capper admitted to the shooting. McMaster is delighted, but it isn't enough. Chucky must go back in and do it again. Chucky says "No!" He has survived the most dangerous moment of his precarious life, and he isn't about to press his luck. McMaster insists, and Chucky reluctantly agrees to go back in and finish Capper off. At 10:45 a.m., the tape in the hidden body recorder is replaced and Chucky is taken back to the holding cell with a contrived explanation for his short court appearance.

Once again, the tape recording picks up the events. The sound of the jailer's heavy keys clanking against the metal door is heard as the lock is turned and the door opens. Seeing Capper, Chucky exclaims, "Dry run. What you tucking your shirt in for, you fat pig." Capper tries to explain his pants falling down, but Chucky moves ahead quickly with, "Hey, what does that mean?"

Capper isn't sure, but offers, "Come back at 1:30?"

"No, they told me, I don't know when, they had like a little pink paper, dry run."

Capper, having recent experience in the Ventura court system, observes, "The orange is a dry run."

Chucky dodges with, "So that's good?"

Capper responds, "Uh, well, they, you said they had three days to file on you?"

"Well, that's what I've always thought. Seventy-two hours, or some shit like that," Chucky explains.

The conversation then takes a dangerous turn as Capper, who knows his way around the custody section of the courthouse asks, "Why'd they take you that way?"

Chucky, thinking and talking fast, says, "That baboso [dumbass] told, I told, don't I go this way. Tell 'em what, I go, I'm going back already, right? Um, yeah, I believe so, and this lady goes, well make a left. What the fuck are you talking about! That's all, didn't you hear me? I won't make it in time for lunch man. I'm starving, homie, they won't even give me a fucking ..."

"Sandwich," Capper finishes Chucky's sentence.

Once again of like mind, Chucky shifts the conversation back to other homeboys they have seen in jail and their alleged crimes. Chucky controls Capper by speaking quickly and jumping from one topic to the next without warning, nudging Capper toward his desired topic in a way reflective of his natural style of conversation. At times, Chucky is serious and pointed; then abruptly he will laugh for no reason, or shriek out Capper's name, all to his own amusement. Capper is entertained by Chucky, though it is clear he doesn't understand him. Chucky's aggressive style keeps Capper off balance and dependent on him.

The conversation continues on along the safe territory of mutual friends and moves to a discussion of women. Chucky expresses his appreciation that Capper's wife, Monica, has taken some of his collect calls. Capper explains how Monica is just about done with him, saying, "... my hyna. Yeah, I was gonna do a little bit of time and then she told me the other day, well, you should have been out already, because time is up."

Chucky sees an opportunity, "She put up with a lot of shit of yours, dog."

Capper must agree, because he mentions, "She's been arrested with me and like ... three attempted murders too, homie."

Chucky moves in. "That's why when you were telling me that she used to wake up at ..."

Capper's voice drops to barely a whisper as he explains Monica's nightmares, "... she seen the vato fall, she ... driving when the vato fell like this through the car light, boom, she seen the fucking head blow, pow."

"Oh, right by the car?" Chucky asks.

"Homie, like when she was driving up, I told her drive around, she'd drive around the parking lot. That's when everything happened. She seen the vato and the fucking pinche, she said she just seen the head blow up, boom ... that guy's head."

Chucky asks for specifics, "Where did you hit him at?"

"In the back of the head," answers Capper.

Chucky affirms with, "Oh, you hit him in the back, and then, 'fuck him homie.'"

Capper justifies his actions by saying, "Fifteen of 'em, homie, against ... [and they were] big boys, dog ... they were workout vatos."

Capper's voice getting softer, tells what happened after the shooting and what happened with him and Tony's girlfriend, Veronica Mendez. "I took my primo's [cousin's] hyna with me, dog, [and I told her,] "I'm a kill you bitch if you say anything."

Perhaps not hearing, Chucky asks, "What you tell her?"

"I told her if you say something ... and she said I didn't, I ain't saying nothing ... so she didn't say nothing ... anything homie ..."

Then Capper explains why Veronica Mendez, Tony's girlfriend at the time, has protected him: she went on to marry Capper's cousin.

Chucky laughs at Capper's good fortune, saying, "Oh yeah... she's in the family."

From here the dialogue shifts from the shooting and eventually moves back to their Tony problem. Capper tells Chucky, "Tony's tellin' 'em everything ... do whatever you want to do to him, I'm on your side ... you know what I mean? So you can fuck 'em all, whatever you gotta do to him, fuck it."

Chucky responds, "Man, those are pretty harsh words, ey?"

Then Chucky reminds Capper they need to get permission from the shot callers for any further action against Tony. He suggests maybe newspaper clippings tending to back up Capper's story and perhaps some "clavo" (heroin) for Macho might do the trick.

Capper finds this agreeable, "Yeah ... because I mean I feel if he [Tony] gets away and nothing happens to him ..."

"So well what you want to do, fat boy?"

"Whatever has to be done, you know what I mean, whatever has to be done dog, fuck it because, you know what I mean ... we let him get away homie, he's gonna turn around and snitch on me homie, and

I don't, who know if it'll go through or not, you know? They might believe him…"

Chucky interjects, "Can't take that chance."

"No I can't," Capper agrees.

Soon thereafter, Capper gives his justification for going after Tony. "The way I look at it now, he's, what he's trying to do to me, ya know? And why am I gonna hold back. Fuck him, homie. You know I tried to risk my life over there for him … fuck that, fuck that homie … ya know."

Capper is able to make sense of it all. Someone had to go down for what happened in Lot 10. Tony had made it known he was ready to give Capper up, and who knows, somebody in law enforcement just might "believe him." Capper couldn't "take that chance" especially after he had risked his life for Tony. In Capper's eyes, Tony had betrayed Capper, his own cousin, and put Capper in peril. Capper would do what he had to do.

The tape picks up the sound of the lock turning and the door opening as the deputy opens the holding cell. The call for "Alvarado" is heard as Chucky stands to leave. Chucky says goodbye with, "Alright, homie, be cool, huh?" "Alright, homie," Capper answers. Then, as if he means it, Chucky says, "Good luck, homie."

With that, the wire operation was over. The reports later written made it clear it was a total success. However, nothing expressed the true feelings of McMaster, Jewell and Haney, like Bill Haney's personal note dated August 28, 2000. Haney had memorialized every detail of the operation in his journal, but on August 28th there was only one entry:

NAILED RODRIGUEZ ON FRIDAY. I BELIEVE A COMPLETE CONFESSION TO HOMICIDE. USES PRISON, GANG, SPANGLISH LINGO, BUT STILL QUITE CLEAR. "I DID IT"

That said it all, for all of them.

CHAPTER 13

Do What You Have To Do

HAVING LISTENED TO the entire conversation, it occurred to me that in all my years in the business I had never heard anything like the August 25, 2000 wire operation. It was the most sophisticated sting in the history of Ventura County law enforcement. That it worked the way they planned it was amazing. Still more amazing was the fact that they had decided to do it in the first place. What was in it for them? McMaster, Haney, Totten and even Bradbury had invested hundreds of man-hours in an effort to prove that a convicted murderer was innocent! This was hard for me to believe.

What was more disturbing was the position of the Santa Barbara D.A.'s office. As I started in on their reports, it became clear they would not capitulate. Santa Barbara started a personal investigation of everyone involved in the sting operation, looking for evidence to prove Tony and Chucky had conspired in creating a bogus story designed to get Tony out of prison. Better yet, their theory concluded that Capper was a willing participant in the conspiracy and the Ventura D.A.'s office and Detective McMaster had been suckered into believing it. They were going to trial with every intention of winning.

Realizing this would be a long and contentious hearing was not a happy thought. It meant I would have to spend countless hours preparing. I began by reading the reports written prior to the first trial. In sharp contrast to the perfectly organized reports done by the Ventura D.A., the Santa Barbara reports were all over the place, and certain portions were missing. Without all the reports, we were not about to start a trial where a man's life was at stake.

With that in mind, I gave Len a call. Whenever I had a problem, I called Len, and I had a serious problem.

Len answered, "Yes, Phil," with the feigned irritation he liked to put on when he knew it was me.

"Lenny, the Santa Barbara reports in the Estrada file are a mess. There's no order to the file, and probably half of it is missing. This isn't like you, my friend."

"I know," Len confessed, "and I knew you would be whining about it before long." "Well, so what's up, where's the rest of the file?"

"That's all we've got."

I said nothing. Len knew what I thought, and he would get around to answering me shortly.

"The Writ attorney, Chaitin's his name, says this is all he had, and when I tell him we need to get everything, he tells me we don't need it."

Once again I hesitated, as this revelation was hard to process. Then, "Isn't this thing already set for a trial, Len?"

"That's right, June 4, in Department One in Santa Barbara."

"So let me get this straight. There's a trial set just ten weeks from now, for a guy doing life, where the defense is factual innocence, and you haven't subpoenaed anyone, and you don't have all the discovery. Is that about right, Len?"

"Yeah, that's about the size of it. Guess you now know why I got you into it?"

Not amused, I fumed. It was one thing to get up to speed on a case; it was another to not even have the required documents. It was time to get angry, "This is bullshit, Len, I can't get involved in this. This is ridiculous—no witnesses, half the reports, and oh, by the way, a trial date. No way, my friend."

Len had prepared for this moment; he knew it was inevitable. His response was typically blunt.

"You have to do this, Phil, so quit crying about it."

"Oh, is that right? Would you like to tell me why?"

"Because you have to do what you have to do."

There it was, Len had said it, and he wasn't about to take it back. At first I thought it a cheap shot. Len was making it personal. This wasn't just business anymore; it was now a matter of honor, a challenge to my personal integrity. Anger shot through my veins, and I could feel my fair skin go red as I struggled to find words strong enough to express my indignation. The words never came. Perhaps because I felt Len stiffen preparing for the worst, or perhaps because I knew he was right, and it was better to get on with it. Why waste any more energy blaming my friend for doing what he believed was right?

I hesitated a moment longer, then moved on. "So, why didn't you just get all the discovery from Lax?" Having known Joe Lax for most of my career, it seemed a simple matter to pick up his original file.

Len knew I would eventually get here, so he was ready. "Lax lost his file," he said flatly.

"He what?"

"He lost his file, he's not sure when. Maybe when he moved offices, he says."

Normally, lawyers were required to keep the original, or copies, of their clients' files for at least seven years.[64] To have "lost" a file in a murder case where the client received a life sentence was unimaginable, particularly when the client had always maintained his innocence. I should have been surprised by this, but I was getting accustomed to it. In fact, I was starting to see a pattern.

"So, the only way we can get the rest of the reports is through the D.A.'s office," I said with resignation.

"Looks that way to me," Len agreed. "And, of course, that's your job, isn't it? So, if you want to get going on that, the original D.A.'s still on the case, Hilary Dozer. I've dealt with him a little already, and I think you and he are made for each other."

I knew what that meant, and I didn't like it. The work was difficult enough without having to deal with some hard case every step of the way.

Slowly, a way out once again entered my mind. I didn't hesitate to tell Len about it.

"I can't do that, Len. I'm not the attorney of record, and the client hasn't retained me yet." Hope of escape once again entered my consciousness.

"I thought about that," Len said. "So, I called the warden's office at Chino, where they transferred Estrada pending the trial. I think I can get us in to see him on Saturday, but I need a copy of your driver's license and bar card, so why don't you fax that over now."

"What about his lawyer—what's he think about us going to see his client?"

"I mentioned it to him," Len replied. "He was alright with it, but you can confirm that if you want."

"I think I'll do that, Len. Maybe he'll change his mind." Len hesitated for a moment. At last, I had hit a soft spot, something Len had not anticipated.

He recovered quickly. "I really think you ought to go see this kid, Phil. Neither of his other lawyers did; at least I know Chaitin has never gone to see him."

Len's tone had finally changed. He was no longer demanding compliance. No, he had humbled himself ever so slightly to gain my sympathy, and that was all I wanted.

"I'll check in with him tomorrow; anything else?" I asked, using a phrase that I often used when concluding our conversations.

"No, that's about it," Len said as he disconnected.

I hung up and thought, "Great, just what I wanted to do on Saturday, go to prison."

❊

It was Saturday, March 17, 2001, and Len and I were on our way to Chino. We had brought along an old friend of mine, Richard Hamlish. Dick Hamlish was a remnant of a dying breed of great lawyers. What made Dick different was his choice of clients. For most of his career, he had taken on the cause of the underprivileged. Whether it was a plaintiff against an insurance company, a criminal defendant against the government, or an individual against a corporation, Hamlish was invariably on the side of the underdog.

I had called Dick about the Estrada case because if we were successful on the Writ, our client might have a federal civil rights case against Santa Barbara. I told him that we had a long way to go before he might file a claim, but I would like to have him with us just the same. Dick never hesitated, as soon as he heard the facts he signed on.

Going into jail was something I hated to do. Len would tell anyone who asked that I usually made him do it for me. The experience always left me either depressed or angry: depressed if I thought my client should be there and mad as hell if I thought he shouldn't.

Chino was an older prison, with a series of chain link fences on the perimeter topped with razor wire. We were going into the main cellblock, so we had to pass through three separate security stations. Each station required us to show identification and walk through a metal detector. Finally, we entered one of the oldest buildings at the center of the complex. After passing through two more reinforced steel doors, we were escorted to a large room that had a huge Seal of the State of California on one wall and a large conference table in the center, which took up most of the room. The guard told us to sit at the table on the side opposite the door. We sat and waited until a guard in full riot gear walked in with our client.

My first look at Tony Estrada remains a picture in my mind to this day. A small man, perhaps five feet eight inches tall, thin of build, his hair was closely cut and neatly combed. He had no visible tattoos, and his skin color was lighter than my own, as if he hadn't seen the sun in years. His clean-shaven, expressionless face held a pair of steel-rimmed glasses slightly bent to one side, giving him an older, more intelligent look. He wore a fading yellow jumpsuit with flip-flop rubber sandals for shoes.

Handcuffed behind his back, the guard turned the chair around backwards so he could sit. The chains on his legs caught on the legs of the chair. Leaning awkwardly over the back of the chair, Tony braced himself against the table throughout the interview.

I started by telling Tony who we were and why we were there. I tried not to be too optimistic, though I am sure my enthusiasm for his case was evident. Throughout, the expression on Tony's face never changed. His look was deeply serious as if he were memorizing my every word.

His only response came when I began to discuss the details of the wire operation. He interrupted me mid-sentence and asked me to keep my voice down. Then, I realized his concern: the guard sitting just outside the open door. A feeling of embarrassment descended on me as I came to grips with my own ignorance. Recovering, I changed the subject and asked him how he had gotten by at Pelican Bay.

Tony's demeanor lightened as he described his Bible study and how it had sustained him. I let him know that all three of us were religious men: a Presbyterian, a Jew and a Catholic. Tony almost smiled and said, "I have been praying about it all for a very long time." He even "prayed for his enemies," who were "quite powerful. Some are even members of my own household."[65]

I recognized the scripture, but I didn't understand its application. Then I remembered that Capper was his cousin, a family member.

It was at this moment I surrendered myself to Tony Estrada. Tony had been praying for a man with whom he had grown up, whom he knew to be a murderer, who had betrayed him, allowed him to be convicted of a crime he committed, left him to rot in prison and then conspired to have him killed. In spite of it all, Tony prayed for Capper. His faith astounded me. I would never think of abandoning him again.

There was nothing left to be said. We were retained to represent Tony Estrada in a struggle for his life. Then a strange urge overtook me. I felt the need to pray. This certainly was not my habit, and all my rational instincts fought against it. Even so, I asked if we might say a short prayer, and to my relief no one objected. So, we prayed. I prayed for the truth to come out and for justice for Tony Estrada, and justice for all concerned. The prayer ended with a sincere "Amen" from all present. Then, we called for the guard, and he took Tony away, back to his cell, deep within the bowels of Chino State Prison.

CHAPTER 14

An Extraordinary Writ

HABEAS CORPUS IS Latin for "produce the body."[66] Typically, a Writ of Habeas Corpus is a court order demanding the production of a prisoner before the judge issuing the writ. Historically, a writ was issued when a judge made a preliminary finding that a prisoner's constitutional rights had been violated. Over time, these rights have come to include cases of actual innocence.

Thus, in order for Tony Estrada to receive a hearing on whether he was unlawfully imprisoned, he needed to file a Petition for Writ of Habeas Corpus. A Writ of Habeas Corpus is often referred to as an "extraordinary writ," because the relief it is seeking is exceptional. Lawyers who practice this type of law, appellate attorneys, will tell you they are called "extraordinary" because they are so rarely granted. Normally, a Writ of Habeas Corpus is filed only after the defendant has been convicted and he has exhausted all of his appeals. It is very rare for a judge to agree to review a conviction already affirmed by both the trial and appellate courts.

Tony Estrada's Petition for Writ of Habeas Corpus had been prepared by Leonard Chaitin. Tony's family had scraped together their last dollar to hire Chaitin. To his credit, Chaitin had prepared a petition outlining much of the new evidence of Tony's innocence and filed it on January 29, 2001. After considering the petition for over two months, the trial judge, the Honorable Frank Ochoa, granted an "Order on Petition for Writ of Habeas Corpus."[67] The order granted Tony a hearing that would require him to prove the truth of his petition. Should the court find by a preponderance of the evidence that the new facts were true, the order would be granted, and the prisoner would be entitled to relief. Thus, the burden of proof lay upon the petitioner, Tony Estrada, and his attorney, Leonard Chaitin.

Responding to Chaitin's writ fell to one of the most senior members of the Santa Barbara D.A.'s office, Gerald McC. Franklin. Despite the odd manner in which he signed his name, or perhaps because of it, everyone around the courthouse knew him simply as Jerry. Jerry Franklin looked and acted the role of a legal scholar. Grey hair and full beard complemented by steely blue eyes, his first impression was one of a well-cultivated sage. His manner of dress was informal for a lawyer; he rarely wore a tie, except when required by a court appearance, and often wore deck shoes in and out of court. His mannerisms reminded me of a favorite professor in college, the one who spent extra time and encouraged worthy effort. His easy-going style and quick reference to his opposition as "friend" could be disarming. For all of his grace and polite manner of speech, Jerry Franklin was no friend of the defense. He might lull other lawyers into believing he treated them honorably, but for me, he was just smart enough to know what he was doing, and smooth enough to cover for it.

Franklin prepared and filed his "Opposition to Writ of Habeas Corpus" on April 9, 2001. In it he denied all the factual allegations asserted in Chaitin's writ and explained why the court should reject them. He relied primarily upon the strength of the evidence at the trial. But it was his response to Capper's confession that got my attention. He referenced a March 27, 2001 interview done by Santa Barbara Police Sergeant Don Knapp and Detective Jessie Rose at the Ventura County Jail. In a study of understatement, Franklin asserted, "In the interview, Alfonso Rodriguez repudiated his 'confession' to Jorge Alvarado." The details and nature of Capper's "repudiation" were not mentioned by Franklin. However, a transcript of the interview was attached.[68] Of everything I had seen thus far, and of everything that would come after, nothing would outrage me as much as Knapp and Rose's interview of Capper.

When I first heard it, I was driving home. When it became clear to me what they had done, I had to pull over. Never before had law enforcement evoked such intense anger and repulsion within me as did these two detectives with their supposed interview of a man they knew to be a major gangster and confessed killer.

In a strategy session conducted before Capper's interview, D.A. Tom Sneddon announced to Hilary Dozer, Jerry Franklin and other senior staff that he would henceforth be personally in charge of the "operation." Sneddon told them they were to interview Capper at the Ventura County Jail, but not as a suspect. In fact, Sneddon told Detectives Knapp and Rose they were *not* to advise Capper of his Miranda rights. Instead, Capper was to be informed that "anything he says during this interview will not be disclosed to the Ventura District Attorney's Office."

Incredibly, Hilary Dozer prepared a memo of this March 21, 2001 meeting that we managed to get a copy of years later.[69] The memo and the contents of the subsequent interview made it clear that Santa Barbara law enforcement, led by its commander-in-chief, intended to make a deal with a confessed killer. Their offer was simple: no matter what Capper told them, it would not be used against him.

In return, all they wanted was Capper's cooperation in repudiating his confession. That might seem simple enough, but there were a couple of problems. First, how could they get Capper to believe they were really on his side, and second, could they get him to tell a plausible story about why he confessed to Chucky? This was a lot to ask of Detectives Knapp and Rose, but they did their best.

The interview took place on March 27, 2001 in a small room at a Ventura County Jail. It was tape recorded by the detectives and listened to by the Ventura D.A.'s office at another location. The strategy used by the detectives was to suggest the answer they wanted in the questions they asked. Sergeant Knapp would later admit that he used "leading questions" designed to elicit the response suggested in the question itself.[70] Their "theory" was that Capper was in on the sting operation from the beginning. Capper wasn't the one who got stung, but rather

Ventura law enforcement. Capper had agreed to confess to the murder out of sheer benevolence. He was just trying to help out his cousin and his old friend Chucky, who was looking for an early release from Pelican Bay. So it was through a brilliant scheme devised by Chucky that Detective McMaster and the Ventura D.A.'s office had been duped into believing that Capper, and not Tony Estrada, was the real killer. All Detectives Knapp and Rose had to do was get Capper to "admit" that he really wasn't the shooter in Lot 10 and that he probably shouldn't have gone along with Tony and Chucky on this one. This was particularly the case now, since, in retrospect, he could see that confessing to a murder he didn't commit wasn't a good idea. After all, somebody might actually believe he "*did it*" and try to pin it on him.

The transcript of the interview attached to Franklin's Response told the whole story.[71]

It begins with Capper's reluctance to discuss anything with the detectives and his lawyer's admonition not to speak to them. His demeanor is hesitant—cautious, even.

Rose and Knapp reassured Capper in many ways, first telling him he was "a witness right now, and anything you say here—we're not going to use against you down here in all your other stuff." They even emphasized to him that he hadn't been read his Miranda rights, precisely because he was *not* being interviewed as a suspect, like this:

Knapp: You notice; you notice we're not reading you your Miranda rights?

Capper: Yeah.

Knapp: I'm gonna; I'm gonna tell you. I'm gonna tell you. We have the right guy in custody. Not you. We're talking about; we're talking about Tony.

The detectives continue, noting that none of their witnesses have placed Capper inside the lot, and then pose a series of "hypothetical" statements about what Capper "would" do if he had happened to know that Chucky had been wearing a wire:

Knapp: Now, if Chucky called you or told you on; in, in a letter, that he was going to come down here and he was going to wear a wire...."

To this, Capper just hums a deep, baritone "hmmmm," a pondering, thoughtful sound not indicating any specific emotional reaction.

At page 6:

Knapp: Okay. Did you know he was being; that he was wired when he walked in there? Look me in the eye, man! He; did you know he was wearing a wire?

Capper: [Softly] Yeah.

Rose: Did he tell you that? In a letter? Just; look me in the eye, man! I'm not; we're not trying to get Chucky in trouble.

At page 45-46:

Knapp: Okay. Let me, ah; just so we're on; just so we're all on the same page. Alright. You were never in the parking lot?

Capper: Never in the parking lot.

Knapp: You left with Monica prior to the shooting?

Capper: Yes.

Knapp: You had your own car?

Capper: Yes. We had our own car.

Now that they agree that Capper was not—could not!—have been in Lot 10 at the time of the shooting, they go on to try to explain how he must have known about the wire, and why, knowing about it, he still confessed.

Knapp: No, NO! Listen to me. Okay. We're not—did Chucky tell you that he was going to wear a wire, sometime, to record you?

Capper: Yeah, I know; I know. But, I kinda knew already, though. You know what I mean? I didn't see it like he was just trying to get me in trouble.

Knapp: You mean he was trying to get Tony off?

Capper: Yeah.

Knapp: They did. Who, Who told you that Ed—that Chucky was going to be wearing a wire? Okay!

Capper: I can't tell you, man.

Knapp: Was it a family member? Don't tell me which family member. I don't care. Did a family member tell you that Chucky was going to be wearing a wire?

Capper: Right; yeah. But, I mean, also a friend.

Capper: A friend; a friend. Yeah; a friend of the family told somebody else, and ...

Knapp: And then it got back to you?

Capper: Um, hmm.

Knapp: All right. See? We can figure these things out. It just takes a little while. [Laugh]

Knapp: Were you already in custody for this thing? Don't, don't talk about this thing, but were you; you weren't in custody yet?

Capper: Ummm. [Indistinct]. Naw.

Knapp: Trying to get Tony out? Help Chucky at the same time?

Capper: That's what I; I already knew that.

Knapp: Of course, on the other hand, it screwed you! ... I mean, this did not help you!

At page 58:

Capper: You guys told me you guys ain't gonna try to press charges [overlap]

Knapp: No! No, no; in fact I'm looking at you; I'm, I, I'm; we [laugh]—Hey, after the comments we made about not—we couldn't. Even if we wanted to, we couldn't. After all the comments we've made about not using it against you? I mean, you're smart enough to know that cops can't do that.

Having gotten Capper to play along, the next order of business was to come up with an explanation as to how and why they put together this elaborate scheme. Capper must have been acting out of love and respect for family, but Chucky was harder to explain. What possibly could have motivated this EME soldier not only to devise such a scheme, but also to risk everything by going through with it? There could be but one answer: money. Despite the lack of evidence of a money transfer to Chucky, or his family, the need to provide a selfish motive for his actions caused them to overlook a total lack of proof. Stretching the theory out this far would later come back to haunt them.

At page 63:

Rose: Well, how much money did you hear? That's not that big of a deal.

Knapp: Don't; don't tell us who. I just want to know how much money?

Rose: I'm just curious.

Capper: Well, maybe ten.

Knapp: You got to be kidding me! Whoa. Damn. Who did; couldn't give him; couldn't go on his books! Who in the hell; where did he put it?

Knapp: Ten's a lot.

Capper: It's not—Not really; to try to help somebody get to get out from life.

Knapp: Well, that's true. That's true. Okay.

Capper: You know. But that's not even a thousand a year.

Knapp: Well, yeah, but. If somebody can give me ten, I'll take it. [Laugh]

Having corroborated that money was, in fact, the motivating factor behind Chucky's decision to participate in the set-up, Knapp and Rose are left to puzzle out the one remaining question: just how in the world did this rag-tag team of inmates manage to come up with such an intricate, elaborate plan?

Knapp: I believe you. Right? You know, I guess; I guess this is just from my own. My own. But how did—If you don't want to answer out loud, just shake your head. All right? Did you, Tony, Chucky and several other people, to be named later—not even to be named; I don't even want to know! [Capper can be heard mumbling, "Um Hmmm" at this point] come up with this, on your own, to get Tony out? Just; don't; if you don't want to answer out loud, just shake your head 'yes' or 'no.' You're looking; holy shit. [Indistinct] All right. Okay. I guess I; I don't want to know—Man! You talk about me watching too much TV!

Rose: See, we're just wondering; wondering how everybody got the idea?

———◆———

Knapp: Well, how did you get named as patsy? Seriously! How did he come up with that you would; how did he come up with that you would take the fall for this? And that you would ...

Capper: [Phsst] It's my cousin, man. He knows I love him.

Knapp: And did you kind of discuss that, that, that, that, um, 'I wasn't there, so I couldn't have done it, so they couldn't possibly pin it on me?' I mean, did that come up? Who's the lawyer; who's the, the, the br- Is it Chucky, is the brains?

Capper: Yeah.

Rose: Damn!

Capper: That guy's real smart, man. He's real smart.

Later in the conversation, it's clear that Detectives Knapp and Rose want to remind Capper that he will likely still have to appear in court, and, as Knapp reminds him: **"just; when, when you do? Just** remember, you were telling the truth. Chucky basically set you both up."

At page 87:

Capper: Yeah. That's what he did.

Knapp: And, you know. Just realize, like you said, you got three kids. Do your time.

Rose: That's what you got to think about, man. Your kids.

After getting most of the answers they were looking for in the first half of the interview, the second portion shifts focus as the detectives attempt to get Capper to take a polygraph examination. Capper refuses at least ten times. But the detectives are insistent. In fact, they have brought along a polygraph examiner just in case Capper agreed.

Detective Wilkins, who had participated in the initial investigation of Tony Estrada, conveniently was also a polygraph examiner, and he was there to administer the exam. After all, as Detectives Knapp and Rose would explain to Capper, they may believe his latest story, but the judge might not. They needed proof that he was telling the truth this time. Despite the continuing demands of the detectives, Capper never consents to the polygraph. Perhaps he knew better than to take the test, or perhaps he passed on a sure thing. In part, the detectives explained it, and Capper refused it, like this:

At page 36:

Knapp: Okay? And your lawyer [laugh], ah, is gonna have; or, whether you're represented or not, you're going to have to get up there and say 'I didn't do it.' You know, 'I'm; I said this to get my cousin out of trouble; hopefully to get my cousin out of trouble.'

Capper: Yeah.

<u>Knapp</u>: And his lawyer's gonna say, 'Well, no, that's not a very good reason.' You know, that; you know what I'm trying to say?

<u>Capper</u>: Yeah [overlap].

<u>Knapp</u>: They're going to make you out; that you're either, number one, you're lying now ...

<u>Capper</u>: Um, hmm.

<u>Knapp</u>: ... [laugh]—and, see, we're going to make out that you were lying then. They're going to try to make out that you're lying now.

<u>Capper</u>: Um, hmm.

<u>Rose</u>: Anyway everybody's going to be calling you a liar.

<u>Capper</u>: Yeah.

<u>Knapp</u>: Okay? I; I'm just telling you what's going to be happening to you. Just; I can't think of only one way that we can say that, 'Hey, when we talked to him, we were; he was telling us the truth.'

<u>Capper</u>: Yes.

<u>Rose</u>: 'That he did not commit the shooting.'

<u>Capper</u>: I didn't, man. I didn't.

<u>Knapp</u>: Okay. Would you be willing to take a polygraph test? A lie detector test? We would be asking you questions like, [clears throat]

<u>Rose</u>: You'll know the questions beforehand. You; the, the person that does the pol—polygraph will read the questions. "This is; Mr.

Rodriguez, this is what I'm going to ask you.' And then, 'Blah, blah, blah, blah, blah.' And, and if you don't want them...

Capper: No, I can't. My, my lawyer said 'Don't do nothing.' It's just that, he said 'Don't do nothing.'

Knapp: How about, you go in the other room, and you sit down, and before they ever hook you up, he's going to read you all the questions that he's going to ask you. If, if...

Capper: I'm not going to do it, man.

Knapp: I tell you what. How about if we give it; how about if we leave and try to give it a chance, while this detective keeps on talking to you. I'll try and get a hold of your attorney.

Capper: No, I'm not going to take one.

Knapp: You're just not going to take one.

Capper: No.

This goes on for some time, with Detectives Knapp and Rose offering multiple possible circumstances under which Capper could take the polygraph—with his attorney's approval, knowing questions already, not being asked certain questions—and to every possible polygraph scenario, he declines. But still they persist.

Rose: Then why is that?

Knapp: Even if your attorney said it was okay?

Capper: I don't want to put myself in the position at this moment. I, I, I; I messed up, you know what I mean. I messed up by trying to help him in this, and ...

Rose: Well, what we're trying to explain to you ...

Capper: I understand everything you guys are telling me.

Rose: ... Is that, is that it can only help you.

Capper: Hmm.

Knapp: Can't hurt you.

Rose: And it really can't be used against you. Even if it comes back ...

Finally, Knapp and Rose give up on using a lie detector test to support their new theory. They shift to more fertile ground. They need a witness to corroborate Capper's story. Fortunately, they already have one, but they need to make sure she gets the story straight.

Capper's wife might be a little short on credibility, but she was sure to be cooperative. Getting Monica Rodriguez's story straight was essential.

At page 100:

Knapp: Well, yeah, I know. But she could tell us, 'Yeah, we left. And we got in the car and we drove off.'

Rose: 'And I don't know anything about this other stuff.'

Knapp: Yeah. 'And I really don't know this other stuff. End of story.' That's all; I mean, I mean, basically, that's what we think she's going to tell us anyhow.

Capper: Yeah.

Knapp: But, we need to hear that from her. Okay.

Capper: Okay.

Knapp: All right.

With these parting instructions, Capper's interview was concluded. Not surprisingly, when Monica was later interviewed, she never varied from the script.

The excerpts from the transcript do not describe all that went on in the interview. The written word communicates only so much. Even the tape recording does not tell the whole story. What was communicated nonverbally has been the subject of much speculation. The tape cannot record what might have been communicated in writing, though it does pick up what sounds like pen to paper. Likewise, the facial expressions and gestures used were not recorded.

After reviewing both tape and transcript several times, my emotions slowly subsided as it became clear to me Capper's interview would become my best evidence against them. It was a cross-examiner's dream. In fact, toward the end, Detective Knapp summed up my thoughts perfectly when he told Capper, "Well, sometimes even the best scripts go haywire."

CHAPTER 15

Unlikely Band Of Brothers

DETECTIVES KNAPP AND Rose's interview of Capper had another message for us. It was apparent that Tom Sneddon was prepared to do whatever it took to save his conviction. He had marshaled all of the resources of his office against us. We needed help.

I happened to be in the cafeteria at the Ventura Courthouse one morning when I ran into Bill Haney, and over coffee I told him of my predicament. We had not been talking long before another lawyer friend of Bill's, Kevin Denoce, sat down to join us.

Kevin had never really been my kind of guy. First of all, he was a former prosecutor and a very successful one. He had emerged on the criminal justice scene in Ventura about fourteen years earlier as a deputy D.A. right out of Pepperdine Law School. Though he was not, at five feet six inches tall, a commanding presence in the courtroom, his boyish good looks, quick wit and obvious charm made him an instant success. Kevin was never a mean-spirited prosecutor, just a very good one. All of this was sufficient cause for me to dislike him at a distance, as he quickly rose through the ranks of the D.A.'s office.

After winning more than his share of trials, Kevin found a different niche for himself. When it came to legal research and writing Kevin had no equal. With his keen intellect, strong work ethic and substantial political skills, Kevin made his way into the upper echelons of the office. Before long he managed the entire Writs and Appeals department and, more importantly, became a trusted advisor to D.A. Michael Bradbury.

Then, he surprised everyone by announcing he was going into private practice. Kevin had all the ingredients for success in the "real world," and he proved to be worthy competition. He confirmed my worst suspicions by letting it be known he would only be representing clients who had committed "victimless crimes." I scoffed at this, as I knew it would never last. Competition for business was keen, and no one could survive for long without getting into the mix.

Not long after Kevin sat down, he was fully engaged in the conversation about the Estrada case. In fact, he already knew quite a bit about it; he even expressed an interest in some of the finer legal issues it presented. However, it was his utter disdain for the Santa Barbara D.A.'s office that impressed me most. Both he and Bill were outraged by their fellow prosecutors, whereas I was not quite as shocked. Kevin's righteous indignation was heartfelt and inspiring. It wasn't long before I was asking him if he would be interested in working with me on the case. His response was an enthusiastic "yes" followed by a long dissertation about what needed to be done next. His analysis impressed me, but what sold me was his willingness to do the hard work. Perhaps, this former prosecutor wasn't so bad after all.

After our cafeteria meeting, I went right back to the office and prepared a substitution of attorney making Kevin Denoce, Esq., co-counsel in the Estrada case. My goal was to have him substituted into the case before his enthusiasm waned and the reality of working for free on this monster set in. I faxed the form to Kevin. He signed it and faxed it back. I filed it with the court. It was official. Kevin and I were partners. When I look back now, that partnership was the smartest move I made on the case.

Kevin never hesitated. Within a few days of taking on Tony Estrada as a client, he researched all the law and started a campaign to get all of the discovery from the prosecution. His style was relentless, making it possible for him to back up all of his demands. Kevin was convinced they had withheld "Brady Evidence" that pointed to Tony's innocence in the first trial. His primary source for this assertion was none other than my old adversary, Detective Dennis McMaster.

McMaster, prior to the trial, had made Santa Barbara law enforcement aware of Capper's reputation for violence. In fact, he even offered the opinion early on that Capper was their shooter.

What McMaster had on Capper was his "modus operandi," his manner of operating or proceeding. Evidence of this type can be extremely powerful. After all, if we know someone has done the same thing before, it's not hard to believe he did it again. What McMaster knew, and what Santa Barbara law enforcement never disclosed to the defense, was Capper's history of shootings done for the benefit of the Colonia Chiques.

Joe Lax, Tony's previous attorney, had sought out this Brady Evidence. Nonetheless, the evidence of Capper's history of shooting at people was never provided. Kevin pursued this issue tenaciously. First he filed a motion demanding discovery compliance, and then he filed an amended Writ of Habeas Corpus. The amendment alleged prosecutorial misconduct based on a Brady Violation. Kevin's approach was so aggressive it even made me nervous. I wasn't about to say anything, however, for fear of losing this bulldog of an attorney gnawing on his favorite bone of contention.

While Kevin pounded away at his computer, generating a steady stream of paper to be responded to by his chief rival, Gerald McC. Franklin, I quietly prepared for the evidentiary hearing with Hilary Dozer. Whereas Jerry and Kevin had regular contact, Hilary and I spoke little and communicated less. It soon became apparent that nothing about the hearing would be easy; we would receive no cooperation from our adversaries.

As the last court date prior to the hearing approached, a few strategic decisions had to be made. Perhaps the most significant was how to handle the media. The case had consistent coverage from most of the media outlets in Southern California. Ordinarily, publicity is not a good thing for the defense. Publicity about the horror behind a notorious crime is never helpful. Respectable defense attorneys tend to avoid reporters, and reporters in turn gravitate to prosecutors who are more willing to provide a sound bite.

In Tony's case, we wanted the publicity. Though the crime was notorious, the client was innocent and we had the evidence to prove it. The more we could get the truth out, we reasoned, the better it would be for us.

We decided to grant an interview with a local TV station. During the interview, Kevin pounded on the D.A.'s office for failing to provide the exculpatory evidence. I focused on the innocence of our client and how he had been wrongfully convicted. We knew our adversaries wouldn't be happy, but we felt it had to be done. We had no idea how much animosity it would create.

Shortly before the next hearing, I received a call from Len Chaitin. Earlier I had informed him Kevin and I would be taking it from here, as the client had removed him from the case. Chaitin responded he was "going to take action" against me for stealing his client. I reminded him that the client has the sole right to choose his attorney. Chaitin became increasingly emotional, so our conversation was not at all pleasant. When it ended, I was hopeful he would calm down and let it go.

On April 25, 2001, Kevin, Len and I made our first trip together up to Santa Barbara. We were appearing in Department One of the Superior Court in the old courthouse building at the center of the city. Of all the courthouses I have been to, none compared to this magnificent structure completed in 1929. Done in classic Spanish-Moorish architecture with open-air hallways, magnificent fountains and archways and a beautiful spiral staircase supported by Corinthian columns at its center, this courthouse projects the majesty of the law like none other. The courtroom itself is equally beautiful, with a high ceiling from which traditional steel and wood chandeliers provide light, and the wonderful hardwood tables and jury box provide a mood of stateliness. Added to all this lush wood was a backdrop of long, flowing, red velvet curtains on either side of the judge's bench.

The spectacle of it all was inspiring and, at first, a little intimidating. Our judge was the Honorable Frank Ochoa, the same judge who had denied our client a new trial and sentenced him to forty-one years to life. I thought Frank Ochoa an impressive-looking man. Physically strong, and broad of chest and shoulders, his image was consistent with the picture on his chambers' wall of a college crew team rowing in some unknown body of water. His face was pleasant enough, with soft brown eyes sometimes obscured by thick reading glasses. Though his short hair was thin and graying, he still made a formidable appearance for a man in his mid-fifties. I had called a few colleagues in Santa Barbara to get the scoop on my judge and, generally, he was well regarded. The most damaging comments were that he was too political. This concerned me; I needed a courageous judge, not someone worried about how a decision would play in the press or the local D.A.'s office.

The politics of the criminal justice system is not something well known to the public. The district attorney is often the only county-wide elected official, so his political base is usually the strongest. The D.A. has great influence over the selection and retention of judges. In most counties in California, former prosecutors comprise a majority of the local bench. These judges were either recommended to the governor by the local D.A. or supported by him in the election for that judgeship.

Even if a judge is not a former prosecutor, he must be mindful of the political power of the district attorney. If the chief law enforcement officer in the county comes out and announces a particular judge is "soft on crime" and offers one of his prosecutors as an alternative, that judge is in for the political fight of his life. Tom Sneddon and Hilary Dozer did just that to Judge Slater, ultimately driving him out of the election. If Frank Ochoa had not entered, their strategy would have been successful.

With this political reality, the single greatest unknown factor in our case would be the basic character of Frank Ochoa. That's why comments about him being "political" and a little short on "courage" scared me. I realized we would probably have to do more than prove our client's innocence by a preponderance of the evidence. We had to blow their case out of the political waters that churned in the Santa Barbara criminal justice system. Only then would we provide our judge with enough cover to make it possible for him to do the right thing. If it came down to a choice between him and Tony, like most politicians Frank Ochoa likely would sacrifice the other guy.

Our first court appearance was also the first time everyone involved met one another. We would spend many long days together in this courtroom over the next six months. This appearance, though brief, was quite contentious. We were seeking additional discovery and assistance with out-of-state witnesses. Hilary Dozer was opposed to everything. In the end, Judge Ochoa granted our discovery motion, and Hilary informed us he had additional materials back at his office. The four of us, Kevin and I, Hilary and Jerry, all walked across the street together to their office. Though the day was beautiful, the atmosphere was tense. I thought I would try to defuse the situation by discussing the possibility of some settlement of the case. I naively still held out hope of escape.

As we walked into the D.A.'s office, I explained my offer to Hilary. Trying to present him with a way to save face, I suggested we could call a joint press conference, where I would tell the world what great prosecutors they were for making the right decision. Hilary couldn't take it anymore. The mention of the press sent him over the edge. We had done the unforgivable: we had publicly exposed them. With the color in his face turning ten shades of red, he unleashed a verbal tirade the likes of which I had never heard before. He accused Kevin and me of every ethical breach imaginable. As he continued unabated, he reached maximum volume, and everyone in the lobby turned to stare. He was so angry that I felt physically threatened. With Jerry standing by his side, Hilary concluded by screaming, "I will not! I will never do any press conference with you, or anyone associated with you!"

I guess I had my answer. Kevin and I grabbed our discovery and got out of town. During the long ride home, we wondered aloud about what we had gotten ourselves into. There was no way to reason with them. The more we confronted our adversaries with the truth, the more hostile they became. Kevin and I were stuck in this thing together, and we were up against prosecutors who would do anything to win. At first, it felt depressing, but by the end of the trip we had found the humor in it all. We concluded we were sure of only one thing: someone, if not everyone, in this case was crazy.

Arriving back at the office, I had another pleasant surprise awaiting me. A process server came in and served me with summons and complaint.[72] Len and I were being sued by Leonard Chaitin for taking his client. Now, not only was I defending a man convicted of murder for free, but I was also getting sued for it! The opinion of another lawyer with whom I had discussed the case came to mind: "Remember that most ancient and wise maxim of our business," he had told me: "No good deed ever goes unpunished."

CHAPTER 16

The Battle Begins

THE EVIDENTIARY HEARING on the Writ of Habeas Corpus was set for June 4, 2001. We carried the burden of proving the innocence of petitioner Tony Estrada; consequently, we would be charged with presenting our evidence first. This was the only time in my career that I got to go first in a criminal case.

In preparation for the hearing, Len scheduled a meeting with Dennis McMaster. My preparation for the meeting on a Saturday morning consisted of putting on my Ventura County Public Defender T-shirt. The shirt had the Monopoly game caricature of a man in jail stripes with wings, flying out of a birdcage on the "get out of jail free" card. I wore it with great pride and perhaps as a small dig to McMaster. If he noticed, Dennis never said a word. He was all business, and he was everything I ever thought he would be.

Dennis and Len had the entire case prepared in a binder with separate tabs for each witness and report. Beyond that, Dennis had prepared a six-page summary of all the admissions made by Capper during the wire operation.[73] Better yet, Dennis prepared an airtight response to their "repudiation" interview with Capper and its conspiracy theory. His response was as simple as it was obvious.

Throughout the course of Capper's conversation with Chucky, all kinds of fellow gang members were mentioned. They reminisced about old homies and their gang crimes. They talked of the Mexican Mafia and who was involved. Capper, in providing the details of how he committed the Lot 10 shooting, also gave up the names of everyone else involved. In fact, Capper even gave up his wife, Monica, as a co-conspirator by telling how she was there when he got the gun and then waited for him to do the shooting before driving him away. Dennis proved Capper would never have given up his wife and all the other homies if he had known Chucky was wired.

As Dennis explained it all, I stood back and watched as Len and Kevin listened intently. I marveled at how easy McMaster could make it for his attorney. Dennis had prepared the case, and there were no holes from which they could escape. I had no doubt that this man could make me look like a genius.

Finally, the day arrived for it all to get started. Kevin, Len and I got there early and waited in the courtroom for our client to arrive. Santa Barbara's old courthouse had no underground tunnels for moving prisoners like a modern criminal justice complex. Tony had to be marched from the jail across the street on a daily basis. Each prisoner wore leg irons around his ankles, and his hands were cuffed to belly chains around his waist that were further attached by a chain linked to the prisoner in front of him. When first seeing this public spectacle, it reminded me of the movie *Spartacus* where the captured gladiators were all shackled together and then marched off to be crucified.

This is how Tony arrived in court every day. Once the deputies got him to his seat, the cuff on his right hand was removed so his left hand could be chained to the chair. With his right hand free, he could write on a pad of paper I gave him. Since there was no jury present, Tony was not allowed to "dress out." Each day he arrived wearing a white T-shirt under a faded yellow jumpsuit and white plastic sandals for shoes.

Despite the obvious degradation, Tony always carried himself with quiet dignity. Throughout the proceeding, Tony never complained about how he was treated, and more importantly, about how he was being represented. For me, he was the model client: respectful, thoughtful and incredibly patient. He never once questioned me, and on occasion he would even voice his approval. Most of our conversations were brief. I would feel obligated to explain my strategy and ask him what he thought.

Invariably, Tony's response was the same: "I think that's good, Mr. Dunn," and then, when parting at the end of the day, "I just want you to know, I'm praying for you, Mr. Dunn, you and your whole family." Perhaps he sensed it, perhaps not, but there was nothing he could have said that would have encouraged me more.

As we were now finally going to get started on this monster, a certain sense of calm descended upon me. Being in trial was great; it was the time spent preparing, and the work to be done in between, usually starting at four a.m., which was painful. Like an athlete suffering the conditioning of his body prior to game day, I prepared to the point of exhaustion. Only then could I be sure my opponent would never have the advantage. Instinctively, I knew Hilary Dozer was of like mind. His dedication was fanatical. He had prevailed time and again through sheer tenacity and force of will. On this point, I would concede him nothing. Never had I tried a case where I felt my adversary cared more about the outcome than I, and this would be no exception. I was ready, and now that the curtain was about to go up, I was relieved. I wouldn't have to think anymore. It all would flow out naturally without fear or doubt. I had made the necessary sacrifice so that my pre-conditioned mind would perform as trained. As I sat down next to Tony, I placed my arm around him and told him we were ready, confident this time his attorney really meant it.

At the counsel table, I was in the middle, with Kevin to the right, Tony to the left and Len in a chair behind us. In front of me were stacks of documents and binders with more at Len's feet. At the prosecution table sat Hilary Dozer and Jerry Franklin, equally surrounded by binders and documents, and to their right sitting in the jury box were Detective Jesse Rose and D.A. Investigator Jim Knalls, who would remain throughout the proceedings.

The large courtroom with ample seating was full. All the media were present, with one TV camera taping most of the time. Also present were the families of the principal players. Tony's mother and aunt were there, along with his brother and other friends and relatives from Oxnard. The family of Mitchell Sanchez was present and well accounted for, and then toward the back, in the last two rows was a group of homeboys from the Colonia sitting with Capper's brother and parents.

As we waited for Judge Ochoa to take the bench, Jerry Franklin got up and walked over to our table, picked up the water container and filled the cup of everyone present. He even went out of his way to pour a cup for Tony. I thought it perhaps a gracious gesture, but more likely just good theater. I also noticed that when he poured a cup for me, he filled the Styrofoam cup to the very top. This concerned me a little, as the old oak table we were seated at had an uneven surface of wood planks pressed together by cast iron clasps.

Finally, Judge Ochoa entered the courtroom, and we all rose as the bailiff announced his presence. The judge called the case himself, and then asked me if I was "ready to proceed." I responded "Yes, your honor," and then asked the Court's permission to make an opening statement. Hilary was opposed, but the Judge allowed me to do so "briefly."

As I stood up to go to the podium, I grabbed a folder on top of a stack of folders, upsetting their balance, causing one to slide down across the table into my Styrofoam cup, which then fell over, spilling water across the table. I was horrified; all of the papers and reports would be destroyed if I didn't start cleaning up immediately. I looked at Kevin, saw a look of anger flash over his face, and then, just as quickly, his expression changed as he looked me in the eyes and said, "You go, I'll take care of this." It embarrassed me having him clean up my mess, but I knew he was right. As I passed opposing counsel's table on my way to the podium, I couldn't help but notice the amusement my clumsiness had provided Dozer and Franklin. The thought occurred to me that I might just have been set up by an experienced professional.

As I reached the podium, I looked back to see Kevin frantically moving files and grabbing Kleenex from the clerk's desk to soak up the water. It was then that I discovered who this man was: a team player even to the point of cleaning up my mess. I would never doubt Kevin again.

SHIFTING THEORIES

My opening started with a summary of our evidence, moving quickly to how McMaster would point out the absurdity of the prosecution's conspiracy theory, and why Capper would never knowingly snitch off his wife and friends, until Hilary made an objection: "Arguing." To my dismay, Judge Ochoa sustained it. Shot down by the court's ruling, I fumbled through a conclusion and sat down, concerned that our judge did not want the truth spoken in his courtroom.

Hilary then took his turn. He appeared disturbed by my latter comments, barely containing his anger. His opening started with a review of the evidence at the first trial, which had, as he consistently pointed out, convicted Tony Estrada before a jury, beyond a reasonable doubt. Then, shifting abruptly, he responded to my comments about McMaster.

Hilary then astonished me. He argued that the reason Capper had confessed on the wire was not because he knew he was being taped, or that he was part of a conspiracy to free his cousin. No, Capper was simply a braggart trying to take credit for a homicide he didn't do. Capper was afraid of going to prison, and so when he did, he wanted to go in with a big reputation. Beyond that, so the new theory went, Capper was concerned about going to prison with a snitch jacket on. After all, the Macho letter given to Capper by Chucky during the wire operation accused Capper of interfering with Tony's appeals by telling other homies, and possibly law enforcement, that Tony was the real shooter. In order to prove he was not a snitch, but rather a stand-up homie, Capper confessed to the Lot 10 shooting to protect himself from being labeled a snitch and to further enhance his reputation as a killer.

When at last Hilary finished making his new argument, he sat down with a look of triumph. I didn't get it. Their case was based on Capper's repudiation of his confession during his interview with Detectives Knapp and Rose when they laid out their conspiracy theory. Hilary's new combination, braggart and fear of being labeled a snitch, was totally inconsistent with what Knapp and Rose had come up with. After all, they had already marked for evidence the one hundred two pages of transcript in which Knapp and Rose spoon-fed Capper the conspiracy theory. What do they do now, admit Knapp and Rose made the whole thing up, got Capper to buy into it, and so sorry, but as it turns out, it was all a big mistake? I was astonished, to say the least.

BONNIE AND CLYDE

Trying to keep my wits about me, I realized that since Hilary had concluded his opening; we were now obliged to present our case. So I called our first witness, Mauricio Gomez.[74]

Mauricio's wife Rochelle, first cousin to both Capper and Tony, was living with Tony at the time of the shooting. Mauricio had never testified or spoken to law enforcement.

As a hard-working family man and former Marine, Mauricio made an excellent witness. His testimony was that on January 25, 1997, he had been out drinking with Capper, Tony and the others before returning home. At their residence in Oxnard, Mauricio said Capper had shown him a shiny thirty-eight-caliber revolver that had a broken wooden grip. This was an excellent description of the thirty-eight recovered in Lot 10. Capper showed him the weapon right before the group left for Santa Barbara. Mauricio stayed home with his wife after she convinced him not to go.

The next morning, they realized Tony had not come home and so they began making phone calls to find out what happened. Eventually, Mauricio spoke to Capper who told him he didn't want to talk on the phone, but that if he came over, he would tell Mauricio the whole story. Later that day, Mauricio went to Capper's home, and Capper told him about the confrontation in the Hurricane. Capper explained that when he left the bar, he went to his car, opened the trunk, put on gloves, a knit cap, and took the gun downstairs where he "shot one guy in the head and a couple more times." He said he also shot another guy. Capper remembered that when he shot the one guy in the head, blood went everywhere.

Not long after that, on Super Bowl Sunday, Capper and Monica came by Mauricio and Rochelle's house and repeated the same story, except that this time Rochelle also heard it. Mauricio concluded his testimony by holding up well on cross-examination. The only point to be made against him was his failure to come forward earlier. This, he admitted, was out of fear of Capper and a hope that the police would eventually figure it out without him having to put his family at risk. In fact, since the aftermath of the shooting, he and Rochelle felt compelled to move out of state. Capper's gang intimidation tactics had finally convinced Mauricio that his family was no longer safe in Oxnard.

Our next witness, Monica Rodriguez, was a little more challenging. Originally, we didn't think we would have to take testimony from Capper's wife. In past proceedings, she had taken the Fifth Amendment and refused to testify.

The prosecution, however, had a surprise for us. They gave Capper's wife a grant of "immunity" for these proceedings.[75] This meant that Monica could no longer remain silent by taking the Fifth Amendment, since her testimony could not later be used against her.

Nothing is more common in gang-related homicides than charging the wheel person as an accomplice to murder. Having knowledge of the intended crime and then assisting the get-away met all the elements needed to establish that Monica Rodriguez did "aid and abet" the principle offense of murder. She saw Capper take the gun out of the trunk of the car, and then, knowing what he would do, drove the car downstairs and watched while he shot Mitchell Sanchez in the back of the head, and then moved in quickly to pick him up and make their escape. Bonnie and Clyde didn't do it any better.

Furthermore, should she admit her involvement in the homicide, she likely would never be prosecuted for it.*

Giving a free pass to the wheel person in a premeditated homicide seemed unimaginable. Our prosecutors were betting that Capper's wife would never implicate herself or her husband. They were confident that,

---

* This was the result of the Oliver North case. Colonel North testified before Congress in the Iran-Contra hearings with a grant of immunity. He was later prosecuted and convicted by a jury. His case was reversed by the Court of Appeals because it couldn't be proved that his immunized testimony was not used against him in his trial. (U.S. v. North, (D.C. Cir. 1990) 910 F.2d 843, modified at 920 F.2d 940.)

if forced to testify, Monica would keep to the story Detectives Rose and Knapp fed to Capper.

Even with a grant of immunity, Monica Rodriguez testified with her lawyer present.[76] From the beginning, Monica's contempt for me was obvious. She might have been attractive, with her long dark hair and shapely figure, but a hard edge of meanness dominated her demeanor to such a degree that it was impossible to see her any other way. Fully entrenched in the gang culture, Monica often took on the menacing nature of her husband.

Like most witnesses who are lying, what was significant about Monica's testimony was not what she remembered, but everything she didn't remember. Monica had trouble remembering who was with her in the Hurricane Club on January 25, 1997. She did remember Tony being there, and she testified that he was drunk and causing trouble with the homeboys from Santa Barbara. He even pulled out a knife at one point. After being kicked out of the club, she and her husband left together. She was sure they were parked on the street somewhere, certainly not Lot 10, so when they left, the two of them walked to their car and drove home. Monica adamantly denied any knowledge of the shooting or what happened afterward. Monica had a short script, and she never deviated from it. End of story.

I wasn't about to let Monica off that easily. I thought we should talk a little about her husband's prior record, and particularly, his involvement in the Colonia Chiques. This set off a round of objections as to "relevance," which I managed to argue my way through. Then, the fun began.

Capper's wife didn't know who, or what, the Colonia street gang was. Nor had she known her husband or anyone else to be members. Unfamiliar with gangs in general, Monica did not know any gang signs or understand them.

While I examined Monica, Kevin noticed the court clerk subtly waving him over to her. When he got to her desk, she pointed to a stack of photographs that she had marked as evidence in the first trial. The photographs showed Capper with other Colonia homeboys wearing gang attire, flashing Colonia gang signs while displaying their weapons. In one, Capper was pictured with his wife and their two young sons flashing Colonia gang signs. Kevin walked to the podium and handed me the photograph just as Monica was making her most adamant denials about her involvement with the Colonia Chiques. I now pressed in hard, showing Monica the photograph and asking how it was that she could not have known what her husband was teaching her children. Monica's true nature came out as her once placid denials took on an angry, threatening tone. Her demeanor was now consistent with the character of someone who had been an accomplice to murder.

Having exposed Monica for who she really was, my examination concluded. Hilary wisely had no questions, letting her get off the stand as quickly as possible. At the end of the session, both Kevin and I had a strong desire to thank our clerk for her assistance. She had seen the first trial and obviously had an opinion that caused her to overlook her professional ethic requiring impartiality. We didn't say a thing, of course, but someone must have noticed. We had a new clerk the next day.

NO MERCY

Rochelle Gomez, cousin to both Tony Estrada and Capper, was our next witness, and her testimony was compelling, despite being subject to significant cross-examination.[77] At the time, Rochelle Gomez was noticeably pregnant. An attractive woman, tall with light brown hair and eyes, she presented herself with dignity despite her obvious fear of the proceedings.

Rochelle's testimony mirrored her husband's, except she provided some new details given to her by Monica. Monica told her how at the trunk of their car, Capper took the keys from her, popped the trunk and retrieved the gun. Monica told her she saw him "firing the gun, shooting like [he was] aiming to kill."[78] Rochelle also overheard Capper tell how after the shooting he gave the gun to Gilberto, who then used it to beat one of the victims.

Hilary then subjected Rochelle to a withering cross-examination. She had given several prior statements to the police in which she denied any knowledge of what happened in Lot 10. Since she had lied to the police, Hilary had what he needed to impeach her testimony. Rochelle readily admitted she lied out of fear of retribution from Capper. Hilary seized upon every line of every report in which she covered up for Capper. With each admission of deception, Hilary grew more animated, sometimes approaching her in the witness box and forcing her to read her prior falsehoods into the record. Hilary took on an air of righteous indignation as he projected his utter disdain for the witness. I objected, but Judge Ochoa overruled, which only added fuel to Hilary's fire. Eventually, Rochelle was reduced to agreeing with everything Hilary demanded of her. Her answers came in one-word affirmations without explanations as she submitted to Hilary's tactics:

> Dozer: And, you know, you said you were afraid of Alfonso Rodriguez. Well, didn't you feel kind of guilty that your cousin was in custody?

> Gomez: Yes.

> Dozer: But that guilt wasn't so substantial that you did anything about it during this period of time?

> Gomez: No.

> Dozer: You didn't come and testify in court, did you?

> Gomez: No.

And so it continued until Hilary was sure he had vanquished her. His smug demeanor as he returned to the counsel table revealed how much he had enjoyed himself. I was appalled that the judge had allowed Hilary to bully her into submission. Toward the end, I noticed Frank Ochoa's discomfort as he turned in his chair and leaned forward toward Rochelle Gomez, a gesture that made me think he wanted to protect her, but never did he act on this instinct.

During the recess, I met with Rochelle in a room adjoining the courtroom. In private, she could no longer hold back tears as they flowed freely down her cheeks.

I should have been immune to a woman's tears by now, since it was a common reaction to the terror of the courtroom, but somehow it still tore me up. I felt responsible for her pain since I had done nothing to prepare her to testify. I, too, had let myself be intimidated when I made a decision not to give her copies of her prior statements, concerned that Hilary would accuse me of tampering with a witness. My lack of courage left her at Hilary's mercy since he could use selected portions of her statements made years earlier. How could she explain herself if she didn't remember what she had said?

I started our conversation with an apology, explaining that it was my fault she was unprepared for Hilary. The tears ended there as I provided her with copies of her prior statements and let her know we could explain it all on redirect. By the time she got back to the stand, she had composed herself. In a quiet but firm tone, she explained why she had to lie to the police while Capper was still out, running the streets.

Dunn: Now, as we pointed out on cross-examination, did you tell her [the officer] about what Alfonso Rodriguez had told you earlier in the day?

Gomez: No.

Dunn: Why not?

Gomez: I was afraid and I was in shock, and my little girl was scared.

Dunn: Well, why were you afraid?

Gomez: I was afraid of what could happen if I say anything.

Dunn: Can you be more specific?

Gomez: Well, I mean, I could get hurt. My family could get hurt.

Dunn: Why?

Gomez: If you tell or if you say something, if you tell on someone.

Dunn: Were you afraid of somebody specific?

———◈———

Gomez: Alfonso Rodriguez.

Dunn: Explain to us why you felt that way about him.

———◈———

Gomez: I know—I know what he's capable of doing, because I know what he has done in the past.

———◈———

Dunn: Can you give me any specifics of what you knew about?

Gomez: Drive-bys, beating up people.

Dunn: Where did you get that information from?

Gomez: Himself. Another relative, when he was going to court and trial for it, he would be arrested for it.[79]

Despite the fact Hilary had proven Rochelle Gomez lied to the police, by the time she finished testifying everyone knew why. Capper, that's why. Her deceptions born of fear of her notorious cousin made sense when seen through her eyes. As she stepped down from the witness stand, I realized how fortunate we were that Capper was still in custody. If he had been on the street, we surely would have lost some of our best witnesses.

MAD DOGGING

At the end of the day's proceedings, Len, Kevin and I packed up all the binders and reports that we had to carry in large briefcases back to the parking garage. Organizing it took a while, and since we usually went to the end of the day, most of the courthouse was shut down. By the time we got outside, everyone was gone for the day, except for our friends from Colonia. With each day that passed, the number of Chiques homeboys waiting for us along the sidewalk leaving the courthouse increased. The tactic, commonly known as "mad dogging," is designed to intimidate witnesses, and the lawyers if possible, with the level of threat to increase until it serves its purpose. In the vast majority of gang cases, the witnesses and lawyers that need protection are part of the prosecution's case. Local law enforcement works with the D.A.'s office to provide security, and the law is anyone on probation in a gang case can be excluded from the courthouse grounds. This makes it possible to detain, question or even arrest any gang banger near the courthouse. We were offered no such assistance, so we were on our own.

After hearing Rochelle Gomez testify about what she had been put through and listening to Hilary attack her for lying to protect her family, I was reaching the breaking point. We all have a way of going over the edge, and mine is to slip into a state of rage. As we left the courthouse, I led the way through the gauntlet of gang bangers lining the sidewalk. Out front for Colonia was Capper's brother, Franco, and as soon as I started down the center of the sidewalk, Franco stepped in front of me, forcing me to either step away or step into him. Seeing this, I swung my briefcase back, building momentum for a shot to Franco's midsection. Catching my eyes, I could see Franco got it, because just as my briefcase swung forward, he stepped back out of my way and let us pass.

On the ride home, Kevin and I were of the opinion that we might want to say something to the bailiffs. Len just laughed and shamed us for being wimps, adding that we needed to "man up." Len was always so tough, I thought. Was it because he had already seen it all, or because he had nothing to lose? I couldn't decide which. Just the same, Kevin went home that night, changed the address on his house and bought a shotgun.

The star witness for the next day was Detective Dennis McMaster, but before Dennis could go on, we had a few fireworks in the courtroom. Hilary had been making motions and issuing subpoenas to both the Ventura D.A.'s office and the Oxnard Police Department. He was accusing them of withholding discovery from him. Hilary audaciously alleged that the whole writ proceeding was their fault for not informing him sooner, or more completely, of all the information they had. There was also an inference that what had occurred was a direct violation of the "blue code." Fellow law enforcement had gone against their brethren in another county, and to make it worse, they had given it to the defense without his permission: an unpardonable sin.

Hilary rose to new levels of rage over the issue. He had pulled an Oxnard Police Captain and a supervisor of the Ventura D.A.'s office into court, demanding they give him everything ever written on the case. This was opposed by the Ventura D.A.'s office since not every note, memo, or recorded thought is discoverable. Eventually, Judge Ochoa had to review it all and decide what should be turned over. Hilary did receive additional discovery, but none of it helped his case. Other materials were determined to be "work product"[80] and thus privileged and withheld.

Rumor had it that within all the documents was a lengthy memo from Bill Haney to his supervisor that researched the ethical obligations of a prosecutor when confronted with the facts of the Estrada case. It concluded unequivocally that despite the fact their colleagues in Santa Barbara had jurisdiction over the matter, when there is substantial evidence of innocence uncovered by another D.A.'s office, their ethical obligation is to give it to the defense. To do otherwise would be unethical and likely perpetuate a miscarriage of justice. The memo was work product, so it was not turned over by Judge Ochoa, but he must have read it just the same.

TRUE DETECTIVE

Kevin was responsible for taking the testimony of Detective McMaster, our expert witness.[81] I sat back and enjoyed the show. Perfectly arranged and choreographed, it was without defect. No detail in support of our case went unmentioned. It started with a review of McMaster's substantial credentials, and in particular his expertise on the criminal street gang known as the Colonia Chiques, none of which Hilary dared object to since he had done the same with McMaster in Tony's original trial.

Thereafter, McMaster dissected the wire operation with precise detail. He knew all of the players mentioned and their history of gang involvement. He was able to explain the language used and apply the content to the facts of our case. McMaster concluded with his considered opinion that the tape was authentic and the events described were accurate.

Then, Kevin went on to drive the nail home. He provided his expert a series of hypothetical questions, which were the various alternative theories, presented by the prosecution. Over strenuous objection, McMaster was allowed to shred their theories in what increasingly became a mocking tone. His disdain for the absurdity of their arguments was obvious. His first target was the conspiracy theory, which they now appeared to have abandoned, but was still their official response. The thought that a major gangster on his way to prison would knowingly give up other gangsters, members of the Mexican Mafia and even his own wife was absurd.

Equally stupid was the idea that Capper would lie to Chucky, a soldier in the Mexican Mafia, about a crime he didn't commit. The commission of violent crimes is a badge of honor among serious gangsters. Lying about someone else's crime violated gangster code and would have easily been proven false by the other homies in Lot 10. That would have made Capper a punk, a man totally without stature or respect and was something Capper would never do, particularly since he knew he was on his way to prison.

When Kevin finally finished his direct of McMaster, Hilary shot to his feet to begin his cross-examination. Hilary's contempt for McMaster was apparent from the beginning. He had prepared long and hard for McMaster's cross-examination and he was not about to let him off easily. McMaster must be punished for violating the sacred blue code.

When the Santa Barbara D.A.'s office first learned of McMaster's investigation, they embarked on one of their own, ostensibly for the purpose of checking out McMaster's new information. In reality, it focused on the people responsible for challenging their authority. Search warrants had even been issued seeking phone records for Angela Rodriguez, Marta Diego, Chucky's mother and a prison where Chucky had been held. The probable cause for the warrants was Capper's repudiation interview and the conspiracy theory it created. The conspiracy theory assumed everyone involved had called one another, even Detective McMaster. They even investigated McMaster personally, looking for anything they could use to discredit him.

Santa Barbara investigators had been sent to Pelican Bay to confirm McMaster's interview of Chucky and to get information on how it was conducted. Oxnard Detective Joe Chase, who had accompanied McMaster to Pelican Bay, was subjected to a "cold" interview set up by his former partner, now an investigator for the Santa Barbara D.A.'s office.[82] Any member of Santa Barbara law enforcement who had previous contact with McMaster was interviewed and asked to prepare a report. Most of these reports produced little of substance, but inevitably they concluded with a comment that everyone present felt McMaster's information was unreliable and that they were convinced Tony Estrada was the shooter.

Armed with the results of their investigation, Hilary now set out to discredit fellow law enforcement. He contended McMaster was a rogue cop who had set off on a wild goose chase outside of his jurisdiction. He portrayed McMaster as an out-of-control cop who had found the pot of gold he was looking for at the end of some fairy tale only he believed in.

Hilary's cross-examination of McMaster went on for the better part of three days and it took its toll on McMaster. Not that Dennis ever gave Hilary anything he could use—no, far from it. Patient at first, McMaster tried to win Hilary over, but this only enraged him. McMaster was the ultimate source of all of Hilary's anguish, and whether McMaster was right or not was not the issue. McMaster had usurped Hilary's authority and betrayed him and all of Santa Barbara law enforcement. This was the accusation Hilary could hang on McMaster, and he intended to make it stick.

One day, about half way through his cross-examination, we all had lunch with Dennis. Len knew his old friend was hurting. Having suffered a serious neck injury on the job, Dennis was contemplating retirement, as he could not suffer the pain without medication.

"I don't know how much longer I can do this, Len. Sometimes when it gets so bad I just kinda black out."

"So why don't you take some of that shit they gave you? It helps, doesn't it?" Len offered.

"No! I can't do that; it clouds my thinking. I won't give in to him." With that, Dennis rolled his neck around from shoulder to shoulder, and resolved to see it through to the end.

McMaster only got stronger as he finally lost patience with Hilary. His responses took on a mocking tone, the message being, "How is it possible that you don't get it?" Hilary, exhausted, finally let McMaster go, much to everyone's relief. The sideshow was over; the trial could finally move forward.

ALL IN WITH CAPPER

Midway through McMaster's testimony, the sheriff's deputies asked the Court if we might take a witness out of order. The witness had been transported from state prison, and his presence in the jail was causing problems. The witness had to be separated from the main jail population due to the nature of his crimes. His name was Alfonso "Capper" Rodriguez.

We agreed to take Capper out of order since we were sure he wouldn't testify. His lawyer, Jim Crowder, would have him take the Fifth. Then, we could get his statement during the wire operation admitted into evidence.[83] All we had to do was put him on the stand, ask him a few leading questions, have him refuse to answer, and excuse him from the proceeding. Simple enough, I thought.

I had never seen Capper, this man I had heard so much about. He was escorted into court by two deputies, one on either side. Over six feet two inches tall, broad of chest and shoulders and weighing more than two hundred and fifty pounds, chained around the waist and legs, he looked like some great beast barely controlled by the lesser humans around him. Capper's entire demeanor was one of contained arrogance.

He left me with the thought that but for the chains that bound him and the armed deputies, one of us would soon be injured or dead. What impressed me most about Capper was the magnificently sinister expression on his face. Even behind metal-rimmed glasses, looking into Capper's eyes, I could tell he was a serious gangster.

As they walked Capper up to the witness stand, he slowly passed in front of our table. As he did, he looked down at Tony and winked. Tony offered no response, but continued to watch Capper wherever he went in the courtroom.

As Capper settled into the witness chair, I prepared for a brief series of questions. Jim Crowder stood with his client, and I had no doubt he would have Capper take the Fifth. Then, Hilary dropped another tactical bomb on us. He stood up, walked over to our table, dropped some paperwork on us, and then headed for the clerk's table. As he did so, he announced that he would be giving Capper a grant of immunity.

This was not to be believed. It was incomprehensible that a prosecutor would give immunity to a man who had confessed to murder. His wife was one thing, but immunity for Capper was unthinkable.

Typically, immunity is only granted to a witness giving critical information about some larger crime in a very significant prosecution. Even then, the information is carefully scrutinized to verify its accuracy so the prosecution isn't embarrassed by some con artist looking for a deal with a made-up story. Since the risk to the prosecution is great, and the potential for embarrassment real, the decision to grant immunity has to be approved at the top levels of a prosecutor's office. That would be District Attorney Tom Sneddon.

Granting Capper immunity could mean only one thing: Tom Sneddon would do anything, including giving a pass to a confessed murderer, to win this hearing. I wondered then, as I wonder today, what possibly could have motivated the man. What was so important about this one conviction to cause a sitting district attorney to give immunity to a confessed killer?

We were not the only ones surprised by this latest stunt. Both Jim Crowder and Judge Ochoa were taken aback. We soon decided to bring Capper back another day, so we could consider the implications of it all.

For me, it meant preparing a cross-examination of a notorious gangster and admitted killer.

When court ended that day, Len and I drove straight over to Jim Crowder's office. I had known Jim as a colleague for many years. Len waited for me in his black seven series BMW in Crowder's driveway while we spoke in his office. I told Jim about the hearing and what I thought Hilary was up to. Crowder couldn't commit himself, but I knew he wouldn't do anything that would put his client at risk. He would find a way to protect him from both the prosecution and me.

Our conversation lasted perhaps twenty minutes. When I walked out of the office, I looked across the street toward the courthouse, and there was Hilary, with two of his investigators. Hilary was talking on a cell phone and the investigators were standing by. When I got to the car, Len told me they had been watching the office ever since I went in. Len thought it was funny, but I was happy we were on our way out of town.

It would be a few days before the hearing would resume. This allowed me to carefully prepare Capper's examination. When Capper finally sat down in the witness box on June 12, 2001, I began with a question Senator Joseph McCarthy would have been proud of: "Mr. Rodriguez, are you now, or have you ever been, a member of a criminal street gang located in Oxnard, California known as the Colonia Chiques?"

Capper smiled, and Jim Crowder answered for him. "My client refuses to answer," was the gist of it. Capper had decided to be held in contempt rather than submit to questioning. He might pull a little more time, but it beat the alternative. The judge asked Crowder if his client would continue to refuse to answer, to which he answered, "Yes." Capper was then held in contempt and excused, but not taken back to prison. He would remain in jail until Judge Ochoa decided to sentence him for his latest crime.[84]

UNLIKELY HERO

Next up was Jorge Alvarado.[85] Chucky was everything he was cracked up to be, and more. He came to court like Capper, surrounded by guards and shackled all over. At only five feet, nine inches, he was not as physically imposing as Capper, but upon closer examination I could see he was the real deal. Unlike Capper, who had the look of a great, fat bear, Chucky was all muscle, carefully crafted by hundreds of hours of pushups, sit ups and squats done on the floor of his cell. Chucky's legs were short and powerful, and his chest and shoulders were so broad he had the look of a male lion in his prime. As he walked to the witness stand, he did so with short, slow strides, never once causing the chains around his ankles to come tight. As he moved past counsel table, I noticed he held his head high in a distinctly proud manner, never once glancing to his right or his left, avoiding eye contact with anyone.

Chucky was a "soldier" in the Mexican Mafia, and he looked every bit the part. His dark skin and heavy muscles reminded me of an Aztec warrior, the symbol tattooed on his chest. As he would later tell us, he had been a gang member since he was twelve, and then "slammed down" with the EME in prison. Throughout most of his prison career he had "earned his stripes" by taking orders from shot callers, carrying out acts of violence against other inmates who had violated the unwritten code. But he had rebelled, he had betrayed them, and instead of being a part of that feared organization he was now hunted by them. Chucky stood alone, his strength and courage his only weapons.

He was too intelligent to be unafraid for his own life, and the lives of his family, but nothing about his countenance betrayed his fear. He had been beaten, stabbed, shot and threatened his whole life. Nothing had changed for him. As he would soon tell, no longer was he some "damn puppet on a string"; he had made his call, and he had chosen his way out. "Parole, rat or die": those were the choices, and he had made his. If he had regrets, it was not for himself. He had risked it all and somehow pulled it off. No, Chucky was not about to apologize or bend his will to anyone else ever again, and certainly not to anyone in the courtroom. He was defiant and proud. Chucky, despite all the fear, suffering and sacrifice, was at last his own man.

As I got into my direct examination of Chucky, it became apparent he would be a difficult witness, not due to any hostility towards me, but more of a general contempt for the entire court process. Chucky tried to behave himself, often beginning his answers "with all due respect," and then going on to explain how ignorant I was.

What I wanted from Chucky was pretty basic: a history of how they had set up the wire operation and an explanation of why it had worked. However, when pressed to explain details, such as why getting "paperwork" on an alleged snitch might cause the accused to live in fear, Chucky responded with disdain, telling me it was "common sense."

As we proceeded further into Chucky's testimony, I needed him to explain why he had gone through with it all. Instead, Chucky's responses focused more on what he was still facing.[86]

Dunn: How about you personally? Have you ever received any threats from anybody in the Mexican Mafia, for instance?

Chucky: Yeah. And, like I said, they won't—they won't do nothing to me straightforward, you know. They'll send people if they want to get me, they'll do it. It's like somebody, you know, like me, who I was, you know, somebody that would follow all the orders for them, you know.

Dunn: What do you think they might do?

Chucky: You know, to be honest with you, I don't care about what happens to me, but at this point, I don't give a shit what happens to me. I'm worried about my family you know. I want my family safe, you know.

Chucky's need to tell us what he thought was important made it difficult to get through his testimony, but I pressed on until all the details of the operation were brought out. I finally got it all in as we approached the noon hour.

After lunch, Hilary began his cross-examination, maintaining the same tactics. As he attempted to get responses supporting his latest theory, Chucky could see where he was going and hedge on his answers. Hilary, frustrated, moved to more fertile ground. He went on the attack. Someone had to pay for what had gone on here, and Chucky was our most vulnerable witness. The questioning turned from the facts of the case to the personal criminal history of Chucky.[87]

Dozer: And what did you do that caused you to end up in the SHU?

Chucky: Get in trouble. Fighting stuff.

Dozer: Isn't one of the things when you were at Pelican, you attacked a man in medical?

Chucky: Yes.

Dozer: Didn't you attack that man in medical because you knew there was a green light on that guy from the EME?

Chucky: Yes, I did.

Dozer: And you knew that if you didn't attack him, there would be consequences to you?

Chucky: No. That's not necessarily true.

Dozer: So you could have given him a bye?

Chucky: Yes.

Dozer: And that wouldn't have been a problem?

Chucky: That wouldn't have been a problem for me, no. They had already stabbed him that day.

I was now faced with a dilemma that pained me terribly. Hilary was going to have Chucky incriminate himself as many times as possible. Chucky wasn't going to lie about it. He wanted to maintain his credibility for Tony. It was not hard to imagine Hilary getting on the phone to the prosecutor's office in Crescent City where Pelican Bay is located and telling them that a former inmate had just confessed to an assault in their prison. Chucky's leniency agreement did not cover new prosecutions in other counties. Hilary wanted to send Chucky back to prison forever with an enormous snitch jacket on.

I desperately wanted to object and demand that the court appoint Chucky an attorney to advise him on his right against self-incrimination, but I hesitated. Taking the Fifth would taint Chucky's testimony. My heart said protect him, but my professional ethics insisted that I remember that Tony Estrada, and only he, was my client. No, I too would leave Chucky twisting in the breeze; he would have to deal with Hilary Dozer alone.

Deal with him he did. Chucky knew what Hilary was up to, but he had made his call. There was no turning back now. Chucky never believed anything would work out for him anyway—he couldn't afford to. If it all turned ugly, it would be no surprise to him. Nobody ever gave him a break and certainly not anyone who was part of the system. Business as usual, taken down by the man again. Chucky responded the only way he knew how: he fought back. He may have been going bare-knuckled against a knife again, but he'd taken on the odds before. Chucky wouldn't go down easily.[88]

Dozer: In spite of all that you tried to tell those officers what you remembered what had taken place during that wire. I mean, you weren't trying to lie to them, were you?

Chucky: No. No. My last thing I want to do is lie.

Dozer: Okay. And you come in here and you've listened to some of the transcript, you've listened to the tape of the transcript.

Chucky: I passed the lie detector test. What else do you want?

Judge Ochoa: Listen to the question. See if you can focus on this.

Chucky: You're still calling me a liar, man.

Dozer: I'm not calling you anything, sir.

Chucky: Sure you are, man.

Dozer: I'm just asking the questions.

Chucky: Sure you are.

As it went on, Chucky grew bolder. So much so, that at one point, after being questioned for hours, Chucky told the judge he had a few of his own.[89]

Chucky: I got a question that's been itching me since the whole thing started, honestly. If you guys could answer me honestly, you know, I'd appreciate it.

Judge Ochoa: What's your question?

Chucky: Why the hell did they make me take all these lie detector tests if they ain't going to use them?

Judge Ochoa: That's a good question but I'm not sure—

Chucky: I got another question.

Judge Ochoa: Mr. Alvarado, I really can't answer that, okay, so let's try to stick with the program here.

Chucky: With all due respect, I thought that was concerning this. They kept on asking me questions about this. They wanted to know certain things, and I just took another one Saturday and I passed it.

Judge Ochoa: In short, let me tell you that it may mean something to them, but it's not something that can be considered here in court.

Chucky: I understand. I understand that with all due respect, but I just want to know why they had me sitting there for hours taking these tests if they're not going to use them. Why? For their little pleasure, or what's going on here? I want to know why he went over there and lied to me saying all this, just to have me take this test and they're not going to use them.

Judge Ochoa: Okay. I can't answer that for you.

Chucky: Can they answer me? Can they answer it?

Chucky never got his answer, but he had made his point, and it was one he wasn't going to let go. He brought it up again, and this time he gave Hilary a little advice.[90]

Chucky: How come you guys don't bring up that polygraph that I just took Saturday? You guys don't mention that. I passed it. I don't know why, you know. Man, you know.

Chucky had turned to the jury box where Investigator Knalls and Detective Rose were seated in order to address them, accusingly, before turning to face Dozer and finally demanded, with total contempt, *"Just give it up now, man."*

Chucky was taunting Hilary. Hilary had made it personal, and Chucky had risen to the occasion.

Hilary now pressed in where he knew Chucky was most vulnerable. He questioned him about his family and their criminal background. Chucky had spoken to them from prison, and Hilary had subpoenaed the tape recordings. Some of the conversations had mentioned drug transactions, and Hilary couldn't resist getting uglier.[91]

Dozer: Isn't this the mother you were asking to help you with drug deals while you were still in [prison]?

Chucky: Yeah, it was.

Hilary used this line to delve into detailed questioning about Chucky's drug business with his mother. Citing conversations Chucky had with his mother on a recorded prison phone line, Dozer took apart their conversations about where to hide drugs, how much to charge for the drugs, and so forth. On each statement, Dozer used the preface, "Isn't this the same mother you..." and then filled in the blank with whatever nefarious transaction they'd done. And on each point, Chucky would affirm, thus allowing the prosecutor to drag him and his mother through the mud to make his point. Chucky, among other things, was a drug dealer, but he wasn't a coward. This led to Dozer's last move:

Dozer: And you suggested to her that you put it [heroin] in some ground beef in the refrigerator or freezer?

Chucky: Yeah.

Dozer: Why did you do that?

Chucky: Why not?

Dozer: Okay. I guess that's a good answer. Why not? So you were worried that your mother would have a bad opinion of you. This is a mother you are engaging in narcotics transactions with?

Chucky: Yeah. Cause I'm going to tell you why.

Dozer: Good.

Chucky: Because the way—being a rat you know, I didn't know how she was going to look at me or my sister was going to look at me, if they're going to look down on me, that's why I did that. That's why I told them about—I told them that I got into trouble or what not, so I didn't want them—the way I'd seen it was it would be better if I told them that I got into trouble in prison than to tell them that I'm a fucking rat. Yeah, mom, I'm a rat. Yes, sis, I'm a rat.

Dozer had struck his cruelest blow just as he neared the end of his cross-examination. He concluded with a last shot in the dark.[92]

Dozer: So you worried about your reputation, about what they would think about you right?

Chucky: Yes, I was.

Dozer: And because of that you lied to them, didn't you?

Chucky: I lied to them?

Dozer: Yeah. All this stuff about Pelican.

Chucky: Yeah, but I ain't lying about this, man.

Dozer: Well, is that the same thing like with Alfonso [Capper], you put the pressure on him, he was worried about his reputation, he lied to you?

Chucky: How in the fuck is he going to lie?

Hilary had taken his best shot and missed. He may have hurt Chucky, but he never laid a hand on Tony. Chucky saw to that, and he still had some fight left in him. As we concluded for the noon hour, Chucky had one final comment for Hilary, off the record:

Chucky: Hilary Dozer, Hilary—what kind of name is that? What, did your parents hate you?

Even the Judge had to break a smile on that one. In an unfair, ugly fight, Chucky landed some cheap shots of his own.

When we came back for the afternoon, I noticed Capper's parents, brothers and assorted "homies" from the neighborhood were sitting in the back of the courtroom. I never paid attention to them and was only reminded of their presence at the end of each day when they hung around waiting for us to leave. No doubt Chucky was aware of their presence and their futile attempt to intimidate him. Toward the end, I gave Chucky a chance to express himself on it all.[93]

Dunn: "OK. Now it's clear that you've been through a lot as a result of all of this, Mr. Alvarado. What I want to ask you in conclusion here is, that you made an agreement with the Ventura D.A.'s office to have a reduction in your sentence in this case. Can you tell me if that was the only reason why you did what you did as far as setting this up?"

Chucky, set free, spelled out his honor code for us all:

Chucky: "No. Like I told this dude, you know, with all due respect, my language, you know, but I told everybody they could shove those where the sun don't shine, you know, they can shove it up their ass. I wasn't just doing it for the time, you know.

I would say the reason why, because, you know, that's wrong what he did, man. His own blood, let his own blood go to prison for life because of some shit that he did, man, you know, for some stuff that he did. He didn't have the balls to come up and say, yeah, you know what, I did it, you know, let my cousin go. I did it. Be a man about it, you know.

He did nothing, man. He let him go to prison, man. He let him go to prison forty-one years to life, man. You know how that would make me feel, one of my so-called homeboys would do that to me, or let alone my cousin or my brother?

I know if I did something to my brother and my brother went down for it and I knew I did it, I ain't going to leave my brother in there to rot, man. Yeah, I did it, you know. My brother didn't do it, man. He was there, yeah, but I did it.

I didn't do—yeah, of course I did it somewhat for to get out early, you know, but like I said, I don't have life. I am going to be out soon, you know ... but this man is going to stay in here for the rest of his life for something he didn't do, man. What kind of shit is that? That dude don't got no balls, man. In my eyes, that—that's just a piece of—that dude is a piece of shit, man.

A big bang came from the back of the courtroom, loud enough to make me flinch. Capper's mother had run out, slamming the heavy wooden door behind her. Capper's father and the other homeboys were right behind her, leaving no doubt about their hostility.

Chucky's perilous life was now more at risk than ever. He had left it all behind with no place to go. Capper, the Colonia Chiques, the Mexican Mafia, and the Santa Barbara D.A.'s office: he had infuriated them all. "How can he possibly survive?" I thought.

Having testified completely, truthfully, and bravely, Chucky had fulfilled all the terms of his agreement with the Ventura D.A.'s office, but still he was not released. Rather, he was taken back to the Santa Barbara County Jail and released into the general population. Alone, and unprotected, he waited in fear before being taken to Ventura County for an appearance before a judge who would eventually decide his fate.

CHAPTER 17

Clash Of The Titans

WITH THE START of a new day, our next witness was Bill Haney. Not only did I have a police detective testifying for my convicted murderer client, now we were calling "Senior Deputy District Attorney Bill Haney" to the stand.

Haney arrived with two other lawyers from his office, Mike Schwartz and Richard Holmes, who came along to make sure no confidential office procedures were revealed. As Bill testified, there were seven lawyers deciding what he could or could not say.

Hilary was so provoked he asked for a recess. In the hallway, I watched with amusement as the two sets of D.A.'s argued openly. Holmes, whom I had known and respected for years, was circumspect when I asked him what was going on. His only remark, "What did they expect? He's under subpoena after all."

The epic confrontation that occurred next was best described by one local reporter, Olivia Kienzel, with the *Santa Barbara Independent*. Her description of the event is as good as it gets. In an August 23, 2001 article, Ms. Kienzel offered her take on the day's events, and it reads as follows:[94]

Dueling D.A.'s:

One of the most dramatic days of the hearing was watching Haney take the stand. It is quite a thing to see one D.A. cross-examine another one, rather like watching two titans clash over a chessboard. Prosecutors know all the tricks of the trade when it comes to testifying, making them invulnerable to the prosecutorial tricks that might trap normal humans.

When Haney strode into the courtroom to testify, it was like watching Dozer's self-styled Dick Tracy come head-to-head with the plain-clothes version of a new superhero called the Golden Boy. Haney is young, tall, broad-shouldered, golden haired, seriously handsome and one of Ventura's rising prosecutorial stars. Dozer is imposing in stature and demeanor, older than Haney, dark haired, perfectly tailored, polished and precise in his movements, and cocky as all hell. Both constantly come up against serious gangsters and murderers as part of their job; in their line of work, you have to develop a certain presence or you might as well hang it up.

All we needed Haney to do was lay the foundation for the leniency agreement with Chucky and explain why he approved of the wire operation. If Hilary wanted to take Haney on, we wouldn't object. It might not be relevant to the ultimate issue, Tony's innocence, but it sure would be fun to watch. Hilary, once again, didn't disappoint.

Kevin's direct was sharp and concise. Haney explained Chucky's deal, why it was appropriate and how it all went down. On direct, Haney's answers were crisp and limited to the facts.[95] It appeared to me Haney was holding back, as likely he had been cautioned not to create any more animosity between the two prosecutors' offices. When Kevin finished, I was disappointed. I had pushed for Haney to provide an expert opinion on how the Santa Barbara D.A.'s office had violated their prosecutorial ethics. That didn't happen. Hilary could get out of this one easily, if he wanted to.

It was not to be. Hilary could not stop himself from questioning Haney on the propriety of his investigation. His premise was that McMaster was a rogue cop chasing a pipe dream, and Haney, his friend, had dutifully accepted every wild notion McMaster presented. He started off by accusing Haney of green-lighting the operation without Santa Barbara's approval and without knowing all the evidence against Estrada. At first, Haney restrained himself and even gave Dozer fair warning:[96]

> <u>Dozer</u>: So your answer is, at that point, you made no effort to find out if that was information that had previously been provided to this court?

> <u>Haney</u>: No. We sent it to your office for that reason.

❧ ⬥ ❧

> <u>Dozer</u>: What were the reasons that you had for not checking on that matter?

> <u>Haney</u>: Well, if you want to get into it.

Get into it he did. Hilary got personal, mentioning Haney had been sick, perhaps with Lyme disease, thus accounting for the breakdown in communication. The questioning became argumentative, with Dozer attempting to control Haney's answers by cutting him off. Haney would have none of it.[97]

> <u>Dozer</u>: Okay. So if a person was to call the district attorney's office and try to get ahold of you and was told that you might be ill, and seriously ill, specifically with Lyme disease, would that be information that would be generally correct concerning your health at the time?

> <u>Haney</u>: If I may, I did talk to you, you did call me, you paged me, and we discussed—

> <u>Dozer</u>: Wait. I think your—

> <u>Dunn</u>: Objection.

Denoce: He's trying to answer the question, your Honor.

Dozer: I asked him if that was an assessment as to his health at the time. I didn't ask for a narrative about all these other things.

Court: Go ahead. I'll allow the response.

Haney: All right. Even though I was home for a few days, I don't remember, I took maybe a week off. I called Detective McMaster and I continued to stay on top of this. I confirmed that Detective McMaster was trying to make contact with you. [Dozer tries to interject.] *I'm not done.* I continued to confirm that Mr. McMaster was trying to make contact with you. He repeatedly expressed his frustration. He then told me that he placed a call to one of your superiors or someone who works in your office. It was at that time that I received an immediate page from you, and then [Once again Dozer attempts to interject] *I'm not done!* I then talked to you on the phone, and you expressed your interest in pursuing Alfonso Rodriguez, and you talked about Alfonso Rodriguez's gang moniker, and you told me that you were very interested in pursuing this. This was days before the August 26, '99 meeting. I listened to you and believed you. After the August 26, '99 meeting, I was then advised that you had backed away from pursuing this exculpatory information and I was extremely angry and upset with you at the time.

Haney had used up the last of his restraint. The idea that Dozer, a prosecutor charged with dispensing justice, would intentionally withhold evidence of innocence was so deeply offensive he could no longer contain himself. Haney's sole purpose had always been to get the truth, the truth at all costs, and the notion that an officer of the court would willfully do otherwise rendered him incredulous.

Dozer: Are you still extremely angry and upset?

Haney: I am very bothered by what is gone on here. Very.

Escalating from there, Dozer demanded Haney explain himself and his "state of mind," with Haney gladly obliging.[98]

Dozer: So between August 6th and August 26th, you had a state of mind that I wasn't communicating with people?

Haney: Yes. Because McMaster told me.

Dozer: So you were relying on what he told you?

Haney: His word is gold to me...

His assertion was that he had tried to call Deputy D.A. Dozer a number of different times and that Dozer would not return his phone calls.

Dozer: And after the August 26th meeting, how many times did you attempt to contact me?

Haney: I did not and there's a reason.

Dozer: The question is, did you or did you not?

Haney: No. No. I did not.

Haney did not explain his answer, using up the last of his self-restraint. Hilary wouldn't have it; he wanted it all and he got it.[99]

Dozer: So you waited between August 26th of 1999, and when you were so irritated with me, until almost May of the following year, with the preparation of this memo, to convey this displeasure?

Haney: There is a reason. When I talked to you before the August meeting, I was convinced, although you expressed your desire to follow up on the information pertaining to Mr. Estrada, after that I felt that you had *lied to me*, because the information was not followed up on.

Dozer: You felt I lied to you?

Haney: That's right.

Dozer: Okay. Okay. I guess if you're under oath, you've got to say those things. That's good.

Hilary was stunned. He couldn't believe it. Fellow law enforcement, no, worse yet, another prosecutor had called him a liar in open court for all the world to hear and report upon. Haney had held it in for so long that, when pushed hard enough, he told it the way he saw it, and if Hilary wanted more he could keep bringing it on.

Dozer soon recovered. Though he had taken a serious blow, he saw no reason to back off, forcing Haney to explain himself further.[100]

Dozer: Okay. So in terms of the overall nature of your understanding of his case you based that solely on what was told you by Detective McMaster?

Haney: No. What I based it on is review of my ethics manual, discussion with the CDAA (California District Attorney's Association) ethics hotline, with my own basic knowledge of what my duties as a prosecutor are. I know that when a tested, reliable informant comes forward and says he's willing to wear a body wire to back his claims up, that there is no turning back from that, and I personally could not turn my eyes to that, and I felt it wasn't being followed up on, I pushed the detective to get the job done. I did keep an arm's length at it, because I thought that at some point we may ultimately come to this Twilight Zone type experience that we're in now.

Haney was right, this was the criminal justice Twilight Zone, and we were all living it. Hilary would not stop there, but would continue on for another hour. Haney continued to let him have it, though with a little more diplomacy. But the stakes had been raised to a new level. One of these two prosecutor's offices would be damaged by the outcome of this case. Judge Ochoa would be forced to pick a side, and the political pressure on him had just reached a new height. How could he side with these foreign invaders against his own D.A.'s office? They knew all along they didn't have the facts, but the politics of it all was entirely in their favor. They had bet it all on the belief that the truth isn't what really matters.

CHAPTER 18

My Enemy's Enemy Is My Friend

URING THE COURSE of any trial, certain strategic decisions must be made that lock the attorneys into a particular course of action. It has been my experience that as much as I believe I know where I am going from the beginning, something always happens which causes me to reconsider. Usually these decisions involve what evidence I will present and whether or not to call a particular witness. The call is often determined by what my opponent chooses to do. Typically, prosecutors have a theory of the case, and they hate to deviate from it. They need to be consistent in order to maintain their credibility. This was not a problem for Hilary Dozer. His shifting theories kept us on our toes and caused us to make some unusual tactical decisions, the most dramatic of which was to move into evidence the transcript of Detectives Knapp and Rose's March 27, 2001 interview of Alfonso Rodriguez.[101]

Kevin and I thought hard about it beforehand. On the face of it, it seemed preposterous. The whole basis for the prosecution's response to the original writ was Capper's "repudiation" of his earlier confession.

They had attached a copy of the March 27, 2001 transcript to their response. Now, we were the ones moving it into evidence.

We had decided that the transcript's "conspiracy theory" and Hilary's rejection of it during opening statement was too good to pass up. Using the transcript to cross-examine Knapp and Rose was so valuable that we decided to quietly ask that "Exhibit K" be stipulated into evidence. Hearing no objection, the judge admitted it.

Now, the time had come for us to call Detective Sergeant Donald Knapp to the stand. As a sergeant, Knapp was a supervisor in the Santa Barbara City Police Department. Knapp had been a police officer for twenty-three years, investigating all types of crimes, including "dozens of homicides." He was an experienced professional witness. Cross-examining Knapp was the fulfillment of a career-long dream.

My strategy was simple: get Knapp to "admit" that he was an honest cop just searching for the truth, wherever it might lead him. Then, pound on him about each and every leading question he fed to Capper establishing their conspiracy theory. Finally, if possible, I wanted him to acknowledge that they had abandoned the conspiracy theory because there was no evidence to support it. They invented it, they got Capper to go along with it, and now they knew it was all a big lie. Was that asking too much?

Any good questioning of a police officer starts off with a review of police procedures and report writing. Locking the officer into standard procedure makes it possible to point out any deviation later on. With Sergeant Knapp, it was important to learn what he knew about the Estrada case before he interviewed Capper and what he believed was the purpose of the interview.[102]

Right off, Knapp admitted that he knew Capper was one of the original defendants prosecuted in the case, and he was familiar with his most recent taped confession. He also knew that Capper had confessed to Mauricio and Rochelle Gomez and that the Ventura D.A.'s office believed he was the real killer. Still, he didn't consider Capper "a viable suspect." Consequently, on March 27, 2001 he interviewed Capper as a witness.

Since Capper was just a witness, Knapp told us he had been instructed by District Attorney Tom Sneddon there need be no Miranda rights given. Since they had prosecuted Capper on the same case, it was hard to imagine how they could not consider him a suspect. Sergeant Knapp tried to explain it like this:[103]

> Dunn: In fact, you went out of your way, did you not, to let him [Capper] know that you weren't interviewing him as a suspect in any way, right?

> Knapp: That's correct.

> Dunn: And you also went out of your way to remind him that you weren't giving him his Miranda Rights, true?

> Knapp: That's correct.

Now it was time to find out who all participated in the Capper strategy sessions. Hilary objected, but the judge overruled, and so we learned:[104]

> Knapp: Usually present was Mr. Knalls, Detective Rose, Hilary Dozer, Jerry Franklin and I believe on one of the meetings Mr. Sneddon was also present.

> Dunn: Now, during the course of these discussions the topic came up, did it not, that the wire-taped interview of Mr. Rodriguez must have been a false confession, true?

> Knapp: Yes, that's correct.

> Dunn: And, therefore, there was some discussion about how it was that such a false confession could have come about, right?

> Knapp: Yes, that's correct.

Out of these sessions developed the conspiracy theory that Knapp would later feed to Capper. Knapp did not deny this; in fact he admitted it.[105]

Dunn: And isn't it true that during the course of this interview you asked Mr. Rodriguez just a whole bunch of leading questions about how this confession was false right?

Knapp: Yes, that's correct.

Dunn: And you asked him a whole bunch of leading questions about who else was involved in this conspiracy to create a false confession, didn't you?

Knapp: That's correct.

Then came the answer I was looking for. Knapp admitted not only that they had created the conspiracy theory and that he had led Capper into adopting it, but also that he now realized there never was a conspiracy.[106]

Dunn: Okay. And did you try and track that down and find out if that was actually what had happened, this conspiracy?

Knapp: The best we can, yes.

Dunn: Okay, What was the result of that investigation?

Knapp: We have not been able to determine that there was a—conspiracy.

There it was: he admitted full on that the conspiracy was not true. Later, he tried to explain it like this:[107]

Dunn: But you did in the course of this interview use a series of leading questions to determine, in fact, that the confession was false, right?

Knapp: Yes, I led him to leading questions, asking him—he could have said no.

Dunn: I realize that. But at least in the course of that interview, you were suggesting to him that the confession was, in fact, false, right?

Knapp: Yeah.

Dunn: And in the course of that interview you also suggested to him that the confession was false because a number of other people had participated in a conspiracy to provide a false confession, true?

Knapp: Yes.

When later pressed to explain how all of this came about, Sergeant Knapp was remarkably candid.[108]

Dunn: Okay. And so that's what led you to believe that there was this big conspiracy to get him to admit to something that he didn't do?

Knapp: That was a theory. And with our knowledge we had at the time that was—you know. That was maybe one of the best theories we could come up with.

Eventually, Hilary couldn't take it anymore. As I reviewed each one of Knapp's leading questions to Capper and had him admit that he had been suggesting the answer to him, Hilary let his feelings be known.[109]

Dunn: Okay. So you were asking him to help you get Monica to verify his story, right? And, in fact, you got kind of specific about that. "But she knows where you walked to, and she knows you never were in that city lot, right?"

Knapp: That's what she gave us in her first statement, yes.

Dunn: And you wanted him [Capper] to go get ahold of her, and you wanted him to know that that's what you want verified, right?

Knapp: No. I wanted him to let us get in to talk to Monica. It was almost as hard—without some assistance from Mr. Rodriguez, we were not going to get into the Rodriguez family.

Dunn: Well, how come if you didn't want that information and the question verified, why didn't you just say, "Hey, will you help us out? Let us talk to your wife. We just want to talk to her, okay?" Why do you put all that other information in there?

Knapp: Consciously putting that in there—I was just talking. I have a tendency to talk.

Dunn: And kind of provide the information you're looking for?

Dozer: Can the People stipulate to that? And I can qualify that as an expert opinion.

Oh, this was as good as it gets, and I hoped it would never end. They were miserable, and they deserved it. Unfortunately, our judge was getting uncomfortable. He got the point, and he didn't want it publicly pounded so hard. After a while, he let me know how he felt.[110]

Dunn: How about that, are you leading him along at all there, you think?

Knapp: Intentionally, no. Did I—I guess you could say I did.

Judge Ochoa: Mr. Dunn, the witness already indicated that he used a technique of leading questions. I think I can determine which of those are leading. So if you want to just focus on particular ones for evidentiary meaning, that would be most helpful.

Dunn: Am I wearing you out?

Judge Ochoa: Yes.

<u>Dunn</u>: I can go a long time with this ...

But I didn't. As much as I hated to let it go, I had to. The judge didn't want to hear it anymore, which wasn't a good sign. If he was with us, he should have wanted every bit of Knapp's dissection publicly exposed. Instead, he was protecting him and local law enforcement; this was not a good sign at all.

With the testimony of Knapp completed, we had largely presented our case. Though we knew it was strong going in, and it only got better as it went along, we still had no idea about our judge. His failure to take a strong stand on anything of consequence was a source of great frustration. He was either the most patient man I had ever met, or he was just going through the motions with his mind made up. Not once did he indicate that he was offended by their tactics. More and more, he acted as if it was just business as usual.

CHAPTER 19

―――❖―――

An Honest Cop

I T WAS NOW July 3, 2001, and we had been at it for a month. The case was compelling; none of us did anything else. Our rivals got paid by the government, but Kevin, Len and I were all in business for ourselves. Working a case of this magnitude for free was taking its toll.

I could make it through, but Kevin's situation was different. He was new to private practice and not as well established. Eventually, his partner began complaining about the lack of revenue, so he had no choice but to begin missing some of the hearing dates.

As the next session approached, I was prepared to rest our case. Then Len found something special: the proverbial smoking gun.

After a long and difficult fight, we had finally received most of the discovery. It was hundreds and hundreds of pages in random order with inconsistent page numbers. Len was primarily responsible for reading and organizing it all. This would have been an impossible task but for the fact that Len hardly ever slept.

Len's condition was born of love. His son, Gary, had muscular dystrophy. When Gary was born, Len and his loving wife, Deborah, were told that Gary would likely die young. With their nurturing and tender care, Gary lived twenty-two years, finally succumbing to the disease in June of 2002. Toward the end, Gary was in great pain, even while sleeping. So, Len would rise every night at 2:00 a.m. and go into Gary's room to turn him over so he could sleep on his other side. Gary might get back to sleep, but Len could not. Instead, he would read through every last page of every report and put them in some kind of logical order. Late one of these nights, he came across some cryptic handwritten notes that made it clear they knew about Capper all along.

The notes appeared to be taken from an interview of two women named Juanita and Esther Zapata. The handwritten notes were unsigned and not attached to a police report. They were just there, tucked away within all the pages. They indicated that the two were the sisters of Gilberto "Zap" Zapata. On the night of the shooting, the women overheard a conversation between their brother and Capper. The notes went on to state:[111]

"RODRIGUEZ CAME OVER THE HOUSE AND SPOKE WITH GILBERTO IN THE BACKYARD. HEARD RODRIGUEZ MAD AT GILBERTO. GILBERTO KEPT SAYING 'I COULDN'T, I COULDN'T, I COULDN'T, IT JUST CLICKED.' JUANITA BELIEVED THAT RODRIGUEZ WAS MAD BECAUSE GILBERTO WOULDN'T SHOOT THE VICTIM. RODRIGUEZ WAS MAD ABOUT THE GUN. RODRIGUEZ SAID SOMETHING ABOUT GOING BACK TO S.B.

THIS OCCURRED SUNDAY MORNING AFTER INCIDENT.

JUANITA HAS HEARD A VARIETY OF VERSIONS ON HOW IT OCCURRED.

ONE IS THAT ALFONSO RODRIGUEZ SHOT THE VICTIM, THEN GAVE THE GUN TO GILBERTO TO SHOOT THE OTHER VICTIM.

GILBERTO COULD NOT SHOOT THE VICTIM AND THAT IS WHY RODRIGUEZ IS MAD.

JUANITA BELIEVES THAT RODRIGUEZ HAS MURDERED OTHERS IN PAST AND GOT AWAY WITH IT."

When Len told me of his discovery, I was stunned. These girls heard Capper admit to being the shooter the very night it occurred. The problem was, we couldn't tell who made the notes. A known gangster and reported killer had confessed to a homicide and there was no police report on it. Unbelievable!

I told Len to keep searching, which he found insulting. He never found a police report taken from the notes, but he did find two other interviews that corroborated them. Both were done the morning after the shooting when the search warrants were served. At the home of Gilberto Zapata, Detective Fryslie interviewed Esther Zapata,[112] and Detective Aceves interviewed Juanita Zapata.[113]

The report of Detective Fryslie stated that Esther Zapata told him she had been awakened by a telephone call at 3:45 a.m. on the night of the shooting. The caller was someone she knew as "Capper." Capper wanted to talk to Gilberto. Esther went to Gilberto's room, but Gilberto didn't want to get up. Capper insisted he talk to Gilberto, so she finally woke Gilberto up. As they talked, Esther heard her brother "mention a gun, some type of trouble, that it took time to get out, and that something was hidden under a car."

Detective Aceves interviewed Juanita Zapata who told him her brother had later met Capper at the house. She stated that Capper "was very angry and was speaking in 'double speak.'" Capper was angry about something Gilberto did. "Gilberto had thrown something underneath a car and tried to get it back but the streets were then blocked off."

Subpoenas were prepared for Detectives Fryslie and Aceves and served for the next hearing date. Kevin jumped all over the "raw notes" and the missing police report. Soon he was told there was no report, but the officer who had taken the notes was Sergeant Martel. Another subpoena was issued, and I waited anxiously for the next hearing date. I couldn't wait to find out how the sergeant, the superior of the other two detectives, had somehow lost or perhaps never bothered to prepare a report. The criminal justice Twilight Zone had taken a whole new twist.

The next thing to find out was whether Joe Lax knew of these reports during the first trial. The thought that he had possession of them, or worse yet, had read them and not presented this evidence at trial, was inconceivable, but we had to check it out. I talked to Joe, and he was adamant that he had neither seen nor received any such reports.

———————◆———————

On July 3, 2001, we presented our new evidence, but not without difficulty and over strenuous objection. We started with Officer Fryslie.[114] Len pointed out that Fryslie was no longer a detective; rather, he had been demoted back to patrol as a uniformed officer. Still, on January 26, 1997, he was assigned to the search of Gilberto Zapata's home in the Colonia. As we got into the details of his report, Fryslie testified as if he had prepared it the day before. He recalled every detail. He even explained how he identified Capper as the person Esther Zapata was talking about. Pictures of the Colonia Chiques were seized from Gilberto Zapata's room. Detective Fryslie showed the pictures to Esther and had her circle the individual she knew as Capper. It was him, all right.

As Officer Fryslie testified, it became clear he was a friendly witness. At times, he even led me in the right direction. Fryslie struck me as an honest cop who knew what he had taken down, and the details of it were seared into his memory. He had waited a long time to report the truth of his investigation, and now his vindication had come. Fryslie may have been returned to the streets as a uniformed officer, but he was the best detective from Santa Barbara I saw testify.

Detectives Aceves[115] and Sergeant Martel[116] were not nearly so cooperative. Aceves stuck to his report and offered nothing else. He interviewed Esther Zapata, prepared a report, and went no further.

Martel was the one I wanted to examine. Did the good sergeant forget to file a report about Capper's confession, or did he lose it somewhere?

Not surprisingly, Martel just couldn't remember. Though he was aware of the significance of the statements, and his typical practice would be to prepare such a report, he couldn't recall if he had. He had diligently searched for a report, but it was nowhere to be found. Regardless, his notes were clear enough. Capper had called and then come over to the home of Gilberto Zapata the night of the shooting. He was mad at Gilberto about what he had done with the gun, and he was mad because Gilberto hadn't shot Mitchell Sanchez and John Moreno while they lay helpless on the pavement.

The impact of Sergeant Martel's testimony was dramatic. Not only had McMaster told Santa Barbara law enforcement he thought the shooter would be Capper, but they had taken a report of a confession by him, and worst of all, they had never given it to Tony's attorney. This is exactly the kind of evidence they were ethically obligated to provide the defense, and now we had proof they suppressed it.

The whole truth had now finally been told. Those who were there, who understood it, were shocked, and then as it sank in, they became angry.

My best example of this reaction came from the relatives of Mitchell Sanchez. His aunt and cousin had been regular attendees of the hearing. I had long since learned that there was little good to be gained by speaking with the families of the victims. Understandably, to them I was a necessary evil at best, and an enemy at worst.

When I spoke to them the next day, it was an unusual experience. Tony's mother, Angela Rodriguez and Aunt Marta Diego had started wearing "Free Tony Estrada" T-shirts to court. The shirt had a picture of Tony in his U.S. Army dress uniform with the words printed above. During a lunch break, Angela and Marta came to me and told me to follow them outside. In the hallway, I saw Mitchell Sanchez's aunt and cousin wearing "Free Tony Estrada" T-shirts. With tears forming in my eyes, I thanked them for their support and then quickly moved away before I really lost it.

I knew they were the ones who had the most invested in the conviction of Tony Estrada. Now that they were convinced of his innocence, they had to realize a great injustice had been done. Instead of the closure of a conviction, they had the frustration of knowing that not only had the wrong man been convicted, but the man who really did it would never be prosecuted. Their acceptance of the truth and the encouragement it provided gave me renewed vigor to press on.

Chapter 20

Trial By Ambush

WITH THE TESTIMONY of the Zapata sisters in evidence, it was time to rest our case. When I did so, I felt a great sense of satisfaction. We had worked hard. We had made the necessary sacrifices, and events had consistently broken our way. I hoped and prayed for justice, but I had been a defense attorney too long to let myself expect it. Just because we were right didn't mean we would win. The burden of proof was on us, and it would be simple enough for our judge to conclude that we hadn't met it. Preparing myself for such an outcome was necessary to my survival.

As we waited for the judge to take the bench that morning, I asked Hilary to tell me who his first witness would be. He refused to answer. I didn't think much of it; he had behaved this way throughout the hearing. So, when Judge Ochoa took the bench, I just said, "Petitioner rests."

Hilary sprang to his feet, and so did Franklin. With obvious glee, Hilary announced, "Respondent calls Tony Estrada to the stand." Franklin, meanwhile, walked over to the clerk and then to us, dropping paperwork arguing they could call Tony as a witness. I was taken aback, but I managed to articulate an objection under the Fifth Amendment right against self-incrimination. Franklin was ready for this, and argued that our hearing was not a criminal proceeding because, as he said, a Writ of Habeas Corpus hearing historically was a "civil matter."

Realizing what they had done and how they had planned it beforehand, I got over being surprised and got angry. I went to my feet and argued that I was tired of "trial by ambush." They knew what they were going to do and they had hidden it from me to the last moment. This was just another dirty trick in a long series of low-ball maneuvers. I went on to recite every ethical violation we had uncovered, mentioning Dozer and Franklin as the greatest offenders. When I finished, Judge Ochoa suggested that everyone should calm down (me in particular) and perhaps, "we might give Mr. Dunn some time to respond." We then took a short recess, and I headed outside to call Kevin.

As I walked to the back of the courtroom, the most senior deputy sheriff was coming forward to take custody of Tony. As he passed by, I heard him say in a voice just loud enough for me to hear, "It's about time somebody did that." I hesitated, then laughed slightly and turned to respond, but he kept right on going, never once looking back.

Outside, I placed a call to Kevin, who couldn't believe I was already in need of him. I quickly explained the issue and gave him the cases Franklin was relying upon. He found their position suspect, at best, and was hopeful he could give me some case law before we went back in. Even as we spoke, I could hear Kevin pounding away on his computer doing the research.

Though the issue was obscure, it didn't take Kevin long to find what we needed. It was a California Supreme Court case, which held that under our circumstances the hearing was criminal in nature and thus the petitioner retained his rights as a criminal defendant.[117] I wanted to go back in and blast away, but Kevin wanted to respond in writing. I reluctantly agreed, since it was his arena. I would mention the case, but also ask for a continuance to allow Mr. Denoce a chance to make a record on the issue.

Back inside, sitting at the counsel table waiting for the judge to come out, Len decided to let Hilary know what he thought of his latest stunt. "What do you do at lunch, Hilary, practice goose stepping around the courthouse?"

This was not good. Len was calling Hilary a Nazi to his face. I had been around Len before when he went off like this. On one occasion, the D.A. whined to the judge and Len was removed from the courtroom. Len didn't care, but I did. I was already down Kevin; I couldn't afford to lose Len.

As I started to apologize for Len, Hilary turned his chair around to face Len and sharply countered, "Fuck you, Newcomb," and then turned back to face the judge as he walked in.

For all the things Hilary had shown himself to be, there could be no doubt that he was a man. Hilary was not about to have someone else fight his battles for him. To snitch Len off to the judge would have been cowardly. Hilary may have fought dirty, but that didn't mean he was without honor.

Since Hilary had been denied another shot at Tony, he was forced to call other witnesses. His position was difficult, since he really didn't have anything new to offer and all of the original evidence he presented at the trial was already part of the record. To present it again would be redundant, but to simply argue the matter gave the impression he didn't have anything else. Predictably, Hilary chose to be redundant.

There did come a time when I hoped Hilary might change course. It wasn't long after the Zapata sisters had testified. All of us were in chambers discussing scheduling. It seemed that the judge, Hilary and I all had children graduating. The judge had twins finishing kindergarten, and Hilary and I had high school seniors, both of whom were headed for U.C.L.A. Both Hilary's son and my daughter had seen small portions of the hearing. When Kevin heard that they were going to the same college, he quipped, "Perhaps they will date when they get there." I was not amused, but everyone else was.

This was one of our few lighter moments. It provided an opportunity to discuss the case freely. I still held out hope that I might personally convince Hilary to do the right thing, so I pleaded with him one last time. At first, he seemed to listen, but before long his demeanor moved back to anger. The more I pressed, the madder he got. In retrospect, I believe he had no choice, as he was likely given marching orders from above. Forcing Hilary to see the light only made him blind with rage. Despite the emotional price I paid, I couldn't help but try to convince him. For some reason, what he really believed, deep down in his soul, was important to me, regardless of whether it would have an impact on the trial.

Time was running out for Hilary as we approached six weeks of evidence. Then, he announced that he wanted to have some of the original blood samples tested. Specifically, he wanted the blood sample taken from Tony's cut finger the night of his arrest tested for DNA comparison. Hilary was swinging from his heels now trying to hit a home run in the bottom of the ninth.

His hope was that the blood taken from Tony's finger would come back as that of John Moreno or Mitchell Sanchez. I wasn't particularly concerned about Hilary's latest move. It had always amazed me that all of the blood evidence had not been analyzed and cross-checked before the trial. Typically, in their "search for the truth" the prosecution has everything tested before they make charging decisions. Despite the abundance of blood evidence in the case, only certain portions had been analyzed.

What was suspicious in my mind was the failure to analyze the blood samples taken from the boots of Dino Ramirez and the back seat floorboard panel of Carolyn Wright's Honda Civic. Ramirez had been charged with murder; he was clearly identified as one of the post-shooting attackers who brutally beat John Moreno and Mitchell Sanchez. The autopsy photos of Mitchell Sanchez revealed significant cuts and bruises that bled profusely from wounds inflicted after the shooting. Matching that blood to the blood found on Ramirez's boots and to the place he likely sat when escaping from Lot 10 seemed a no-brainer. Once the blood was confirmed to be that of Mitchell Sanchez or John Moreno, the case against Ramirez as an accomplice to murder would have been a slam-dunk. But the analysis was never done, and Ramirez pled out for credit for time served to being an accessory after the fact.

I wasn't particularly concerned about Hilary's latest move, but that sentiment was not shared by everyone. In particular, Tony was worried. In fact, in my judgment, he was downright paranoid, and I couldn't blame him. He knew how well we were doing and he couldn't help but begin to hope. Now, he smelled a rat. With everything else that had been done to him, it wasn't hard to believe that they might tamper with the evidence.

The DNA testing of the blood samples would take several weeks, so the trial had to adjourn while we waited for the results. For Tony, it was easy to imagine his hopes would be crushed again by some new wicked turn of events.

Darkness again reigned over Tony's life, and once again he met it in the same manner. He went to his knees, begging the God that had brought him this far not to abandon him.

As we approached the final sessions of the hearing, my mood was ambivalent. I was satisfied with the effort we had put in, but I was apprehensive about our judge. I couldn't understand the man. I didn't see how he could tolerate everything the prosecution had done and never once criticize them. If anything, as the hearing went on, he had grown more passive. I couldn't see how he could be in agreement with us and not be offended by their tactics. How could he believe Tony to be innocent and never lose patience with the deceptive games they were playing? Where was the sense of moral outrage in the man? Was this just an intellectual exercise for him, at the end of which he could calmly say he had considered all the evidence, and in his mind the petitioner simply had not met his burden of proof? I couldn't see how he could have the courage to do the right thing and never once give a hint of it during the many weeks of the hearing. No, it seemed to me that he may have toyed with the idea of being honest, but as the end approached he knew what he had to do. Better to protect himself and his political position than risk the wrath of the entire law enforcement community of Santa Barbara.

I tried to comfort myself with how hard we had worked and how well we had done. For many of my colleagues, that might be enough. They had learned to protect their feelings and not invest too much of themselves in the outcome, which was one way to survive it all emotionally. I couldn't do that—I needed to win. I wanted to win for Tony and his family, but more importantly I wanted the criminal justice system to work. I wanted it to work for justice, and I wanted it to be run by people of goodwill.

In the midst of my despair, brought on by continuing doubts, I developed the theme of my closing argument. It would not be about the facts of the case or the applicable law; they were no longer relevant. It would be about justice, pure and simple, and the essential character of those chosen to administer it.

CHAPTER 21

The Closing

TIME PASSED SLOWLY as we approached August 20, 2001, the date set for final argument. It was particularly painful for Tony. Though he never complained, I could tell the stress was taking its toll on him. His letters from jail were often dark and cynical. He appreciated what we had done, but he didn't trust the prosecution or the system they represented. His fear about the results of the blood analysis was contagious; he even had me doubting its outcome.

Eventually, we heard from the crime lab. The DNA analysis confirmed the blood on Tony's finger was his own. Mitchell Sanchez and John Moreno were specifically excluded.[118] Better yet, Kevin had requested that they also do a blood alcohol analysis on Tony's sample. It came back at .23 at the time of the shooting; .23 was almost three times the legal limit for drunk driving. Tony was drunk, dead drunk, just as he had described it.[119]

Hilary had struck out again, and this time the press didn't give him a pass. By now, most of the media had a sense of what was really going on. Hilary had done an effective job of convincing them he would prevail in the end. Most of the reporters accepted his explanations, even though they rarely had anything to do with what had happened in court. He would promise them conclusive evidence at some point in the future. His most recent promise, the DNA comparison, had generated a lot of interest, and Hilary had played it up. Now the results had gone our way again. Most of the reporters knew they had been played, and they responded with headlines such as "Defense Claims Blood Tests Clear Estrada."[120] Public sentiment had finally shifted in our favor.

The days passed slowly as we prepared for the end. I worked on other cases—I had to—but I was permanently distracted. When the big day finally arrived, I was more relieved than excited.

When Kevin, Len and I arrived at the courthouse, it was apparent that this wouldn't be just another day. Both sides of the courtroom were packed with people. Family and friends from Oxnard took up most of the space, but local interest was also peaking, and all of the media was there, including a TV camera at the front right corner of the courtroom gallery. Since so many of the audience had an interest in the outcome, it felt more like a sporting event than a judicial proceeding. Tension in the courtroom continued to grow until Judge Ochoa came out, and the bailiff called everyone to order.

When the judge asked us to proceed, Kevin jumped to his feet and began what would be a very crisp and well-organized presentation.[121] He had charts and diagrams and specific references to evidence and transcript page numbers. He eloquently and precisely summarized our case, and then turned to theirs. In a carefully controlled, mocking tone, Kevin ridiculed each one of their theories on why the court should not believe Capper's confession. With each new "trial balloon" they sent out, Kevin pointed out how we had shot it down with our evidence. The high point came when he pointed out how many times they had shifted their theory, only to shift again, as each new interpretation was proven more absurd than the last.

As I watched Kevin, I could tell he was thoroughly enjoying himself. He had all the instincts of a hunter, and he clearly loved the kill. His presentation made me long for a jury in our case, an impartial panel of twelve, not subject to political pressure, that could listen and decide based upon what they believed was right. As he finished, I thought that we could never have lost in front of a jury, not after Kevin's argument.

Now it was Hilary's turn. As he began his presentation, I was immediately struck by his calm demeanor and appreciative tone.[122] He thanked the judge, and he even thanked us. This was the Hilary Dozer I liked and respected. It was at moments like this that I thought we might have been friends under different circumstances. This was also when Hilary was most dangerous. His raging anger I could handle, but when he was trying to charm me, that's when he was most effective. Fortunately, it didn't last long.

After his gracious beginning, Hilary reminded the judge that he had the full backing of his office and that the entire law enforcement community of Santa Barbara had been subjected to an attack from another county. Not only had their jurisdiction been invaded, but the way in which it was done was illegal. Hilary argued that the taped confession taken from Capper in the Ventura County jail had violated his constitutional right to counsel, and it was the result of illegal police conduct. He reminded the court that in cases in which a defendant's constitutional rights are violated, there is an "imperative of judicial integrity" and the judge should "not want to be actively participating and actively condoning actions which are otherwise illegal."[123]

Hilary had done it again. He astounded me. Here was a veteran prosecutor who had argued for the admissibility of countless confessions, coerced, without counsel, or otherwise, and now he was asking a judge to disregard a murder confession of a hardcore gang member in order to preserve "judicial integrity." Hilary was eloquently defending Capper, or at least his constitutional rights, in order to deter the "illegal police conduct" perpetrated upon Capper by Ventura County law enforcement. Hilary had taken on the role of a great defender of gangster rights and watchdog of judicial integrity.

In further defense of Capper, Hilary reminded the court that Capper was dismissed out of the case by his brother judge at the preliminary hearing after he had heard a "complete array of the evidence."[124] "Well, not a 'complete array,'" I thought, since he left out Capper's confession to the Zapata sisters. However, the evidence didn't discourage Hilary; he was just getting started.

As Hilary continued, it was obvious that he had worked very hard on his argument. He presented every possible detail that somehow could be construed as supporting their case. But what was his case? He never made it clear. He never presented a consistent theory supported by the evidence. Rather, he used the shotgun approach, blasting away at every possible angle, hoping to hit something. He seemed to rely upon a hybrid theory in which Capper bragged about a murder he didn't do, because he was on his way to prison. He wanted murderer status when he got there, and he didn't want to be labeled a snitch. In the process, he ignored their conspiracy theory, which had been the basis for denying the writ.

The balance of Hilary's argument dealt with the evidence presented at the first trial. In painstaking detail, he read from the transcripts, reminding us all how he had convicted Tony in the first place. Once again, he relied heavily upon the testimony of Charles Brodie and his cross-examination of Tony. He went on and on, reading from the transcript as if Judge Ochoa had never heard it before. He had been speaking for over an hour and forty-five minutes and his voice was growing hoarse, when Judge Ochoa interrupted and let him know we were approaching 5:00 p.m. Though he appeared to be tiring, Hilary pushed on to the end of the day. He concluded at exactly 5:00 p.m. with little fanfare and no carefully crafted summary of his position.

That night, I spent a lot of time working and some more on my knees. I was afraid. I was afraid of what I could not control and of what I could not change. I knew that my argument was likely a meaningless exercise, at least in terms of the impact it would have on our judge. He knew the evidence, probably better than any of us, and likely made his mind up long ago. It caused me great despair to think that with everything we had done, everything Tony had gone through and how far he had come, it all came down to the integrity of one local politician. My cynicism was real, and it was based on experience.

When I arrived in the courtroom the next morning, the first thing I did was rearrange the furniture. I had noticed that the podium was placed right behind the TV camera so that the shots of my colleagues' arguments were mainly of the back of their heads. I moved the podium to the center, and back a little, so that I could be seen in profile. It also meant that Hilary could be seen seated between the camera and me.

My closing was relatively brief in comparison to Dozer's diatribe the day before. I had long since given up just arguing the facts; rarely did that win the day. No, if we were to win, I had to touch some deeper emotion, some higher purpose that would justify the extraordinary result we were asking for. My theme was "moral courage": The strength to do what we all know is right, even if we put ourselves at risk. I pointed out how each witness we presented had done what was right, even to the point of putting themselves in danger. Now our judge could do the same, or not, but his decision, like all those who had come before him, would define him as a judge, and as a man, forever afterwards.

At the start of my argument, I took on what little of consequence Hilary had pointed out in his.[125] This was easy enough, since so much of what he presented was contradictory. Then, I launched into an ethics lecture. They had withheld evidence of innocence, attacked fellow law enforcement for not cooperating with them, created false theories and fed them to a hardcore gangster to protect themselves and him in the process. They had granted immunity to the real killer and his co-conspirator wife and failed to consider any evidence that pointed toward someone other than Tony Estrada.

Through all of this, Hilary sat stoically at the counsel table. None of it seemed to bother him, but I thought I knew what would. As I went through the violent career of Alfonso "Capper" Rodriguez, I pointed out how he had laughed at Santa Barbara law enforcement on the wire operation when he heard they had described him as a "peacemaker." More importantly, I noted:[126] "He is a killer. He's done it before, and this time he killed someone, and some day, as it stands now, he's going to get out, and he's going to return to the streets of Oxnard."

While speaking these words, I turned to face Hilary, and when I did, I saw him wince. It was one thing for him to mistakenly convict an innocent man, but it was quite another to let a murderer go free. He had dedicated his life to prosecuting the Cappers of this world, and to let one go and know that Capper was mocking him for it was more than even Hilary could take.

I moved on to a review of the courageous men and women who had testified for us. Whether it was McMaster, Haney or Chucky, they had all risked either their careers or their lives to do what they believed was right. Last, I spoke of my personal favorites, Mauricio and Rochelle Gomez. They had risked the most. They had a young family, good jobs and a bright future ahead of them. They could have continued to stay out of it and risked nothing. They couldn't do that and live with themselves. They had "what is known as a conscience. It worked on them until they mustered the courage to tell what they knew about Alfonso Rodriguez."[127]

> Ultimately, that's what this case is about: does our system have a conscience? Do we really care if we have the right man, or is one Hispanic gang member from Oxnard as good as another? You know how it goes. They're all the same—it doesn't matter. We'll get the other guy next time. Today's victim is tomorrow's defendant. It doesn't make any difference. Maybe he's an aider and abettor, maybe he was the shooter, so what? Or do we have a social conscience that says it does matter, *justice for all, is all that matters.* Do we have the moral authority and the courage to admit our mistakes?

> Because if we do, we still have the greatest criminal justice system in history, and if we do not, then none of us are safe, safe from this kind of prosecution, the kind of prosecution that will continue to make similar mistakes unless someone puts a stop to it. Do what you can, your Honor. Put an end to it.

I returned to the counsel table to the congratulations of Kevin and Len, but most especially Tony. Tony was smiling—no, he was downright beaming, and he didn't stop.

After Judge Ochoa told us he would be taking the matter under submission, Tony had a chance to tell me more. "That was awesome, Mr. Dunn, you said it all. I wanted to stand up and applaud and shout for joy. Where did you learn to talk like that, man? You even made me cry. I didn't think I could do that anymore."

When the deputies finally came to take Tony away, it was hard to watch him go. My heart ached as they removed the handcuff that locked him to the arm of his chair, placed his other wrist in the cuff, and then locked both his wrists to the belly chain around his waist. I wondered if he would ever be free of those chains.

As Tony was led out of the courtroom with a sheriff's deputy on either side, I could see that he was still beaming. Tony had allowed himself to hope again. No, it was more than that; Tony was confident, and he was proud. As he slowly walked down the center aisle of the courtroom, never once letting the chains around his ankles come tight; Tony returned the look of everyone who was watching him. Win or lose, they could never take this moment away from him. At long last the truth, the whole truth, had been told, and no one who cared about the truth could deny it. Tony was not a murderer, he was not a ruthless gangster who "killed for thrills," and everyone finally knew it. His body may still have been in chains, but his mind at last was free.

CHAPTER 22

The Verdict

THEN WE WAITED. First it was days, then weeks, and finally more than two months. It was a great time for speculation about what our judge was doing. One popular theory was that he wanted the publicity and the strength of our case to fade away before ruling against us. I was of the opinion that he was reading the transcript from the first trial, which was almost three thousand pages. He had commented once that he knew the case better than anyone. I worried that his comment meant he was going to come up with his own theory of the evidence. Since it would have been easy to adopt our theory, he must be working hard to rule against us and create an airtight record on appeal.

Len remained optimistic, while Kevin grew increasingly agitated. Eventually, Kevin even resorted to calling Judge Ochoa's secretary (more than once), but each time he was only told that the judge was still working. I never called, not because I didn't care, but only because I didn't want them to know I did. Of course, it was Tony who suffered the most. Whenever he called from jail, I did my best to put a positive spin on it. I figured it couldn't hurt to keep his spirits up even if my own were on the way down.

Finally, after two and a half months, we received the call. Judge Ochoa's secretary told us he would be issuing his decision the next day, October 12, 2001, and that we needed to be present in his courtroom that morning.

At first, I didn't want to go. I figured if we won, Kevin could handle the celebratory press conference, and if we lost, I wasn't sure I would be able to behave myself.

Kevin did not understand my feelings at all, and Len just told me I had to "man up" and go, which infuriated me. After I calmed down, I realized he was right. It was my case, and I had to see it through to the end.

We arrived early in the courtroom that day, so we had to sit and watch Judge Ochoa finish his morning calendar call. I sat in the front row, carefully controlling my every movement so as not to reveal any emotion. I noticed Judge Ochoa never once looked in our direction; he remained "Old Poker Face" to the end. Finally, after he finished with all his other cases, Judge Ochoa looked at us and said he would be handing down his written decision in chambers when Mr. Dozer arrived. Len was disappointed that he wasn't going to rule from the bench, since he wasn't able to go into chambers. I told him that if the news was good, I would open the door and push my nose to the side with my index finger, letting him know the "sting" was on, just like in the movie.

Kevin and I sat in the outer foyer of Judge Ochoa's chambers for what seemed like forever, waiting for Hilary. Needless to say, the tension was unbearable. I sat stiffly, focusing all of my attention on controlling my emotions and listened to Kevin complain about Hilary one last time. At long last, Hilary arrived, looking more stressed than Kevin and I put together. We continued to sit as Hilary announced his presence and walked to the door of the judge's office. Kevin got to his feet first and followed Hilary to the door, while I lingered a moment behind them. Hilary turned and came back through the door with a very thick set of documents and started to read while still standing. Kevin got his copy and returned quickly to his chair to sit down and sift through the pages, looking for Judge Ochoa's order.

When I at last walked through Frank Ochoa's door, I did so with every intention of never looking the man in the eye. I was not about to let this man, who never revealed himself, know that he could get to me. I just walked slowly into his office, my eyes focused on the thick set of papers that he held in both hands, with one end extended out toward me. As I reached for the document, I intended to take it and then turn and walk away, but he wouldn't let go of it. This startled me, and I felt a flash of anger rising up in me until I looked up into his face, and it was there that I saw my answer.

All of Judge Ochoa's professional features had vanished, revealing the face of a man I had never seen before—a kind man, with new, sympathetic eyes and a little sly smile forming at the corner of his lips. Then, a subtle change came over him, so that his joy in the moment revealed not so much his satisfaction with himself, but with me. He was proud of me, and he wanted me to know it.

He was grateful. He had been with us from the beginning, but he knew he couldn't have done it alone. He needed help, and he was proud of me for what I had done and why I had done it, and he wanted to let me know the only way he could. Tears began to well up in my eyes as I lost my dignity, but I was not alone. When he finally released the papers, I could see a small reflection in the corner of his eyes. "Thank you," I said softly, two or three times with my voice cracking, having no doubt about what he had decided. "No, thank you," he gently responded.

As I turned to leave the office, I noticed Hilary was already on his way out. Without saying a word, he opened the door to the hallway and walked quickly past everyone waiting outside. I went to the door that opened to the courtroom and stepped forward just enough so I could see Len, and gave him the signal. Len smiled and quickly got to his feet, heading outside where he could let everyone know we had won. I thought it only fair that Len make the announcement to Tony's family and friends. He had been hired early on by the family, and it was his dedication that had brought it all together.

I returned to the foyer to sit down next to Kevin, who was reading feverishly. "Phil, he's written over sixty pages of factual findings and legal rulings all in our favor, and not only did he set aside Tony's conviction, but he's ordered him released today. He's going home, Phil, he's going home today!"[128] As I listened to Kevin explain it to me, I also heard a series of shrieks and screams of joy outside the door. Kevin jumped to his feet and said we should "get out of here," but I was reluctant to go. I told Kevin I wanted to read the decision, so I would know what I was talking about when the press descended upon us. Kevin stayed with me a moment longer and explained it all in greater detail, but then he had to go, and I was glad to see him leave. As he opened the door, the assembled crowd let out a cheer for their hero and then applauded as he walked out.

JUSTICE SERVED

As the door closed behind Kevin, I was left alone to read the decision and savor the moment. He had written eloquently and honestly. Always the diplomat, Judge Ochoa had avoided casting blame, but rather he made his point by recognizing those who had courageously presented the truth. Of Detective McMaster, he remembered how his testimony had "helped secure the conviction of Tony Estrada at trial," but "when he received information that the wrong man might have been convicted, he pursued the evidence with vigor. When a police officer is as eager to pursue evidence to exonerate the innocent, even post-conviction, as he is to convict the guilty, we have an example of police conduct we can, and should, all be proud of."[129]

As to Bill Haney, he wrote, "when apprised of the circumstances presented, [Haney] engineered the operation and provided the resources to extract the evidence needed to shed light on what otherwise would have remained a miscarriage of justice. He, and other Ventura law enforcement officials involved, were motivated by the search for the truth. That search must be the primary goal of all who toil in the fields of the law."[130]

Finally, Judge Ochoa could not avoid commenting on our judicial system as a whole:

> "The first required comment goes to the very nature of our system of justice. It is clear that Mr. Estrada was incorrectly convicted of serious charges at jury trial in this case.

The fact that his lack of candor while testifying contributed to that circumstance is of little consequence. The reality is that our justice system is a human process and human beings are not vested with perfection. We operate in a system that we know will never be able to reach a level of infallibility.

And yet, the jury's decision is not impeached by this decision, if the jurors had had the evidence presented in the Writ proceeding during the trial, their decision would have undoubtedly been different. It is a fact that our system has complex appeals and Writ proceedings available to correct the errors our system is capable of making. This proceeding is emblematic of the fact that the system works, as opposed to some contrary conclusion. Taken as a whole, there is no fairer, nor better system of dispensing justice anywhere in the world."[131]

This last sentence sounded familiar. He saw it in the same terms I did, and because of his goodwill and judicial conscience, our system had worked. Against all odds, justice had finally been served.

As I continued to hide out in Judge Ochoa's outer office, the party was getting started outside. Though I didn't see it at the time, I later watched T.V. news footage that captured Len coming out of the courtroom, where he told Tony's Aunt Marta, who immediately began jumping up and down and screaming like a little girl before running to Len to receive a huge hug.

It was then that Angela Rodriguez heard the news, and since she was Tony's mother, the cameras were all there to catch her reaction. At first she looked surprised, but then all the emotion came flowing forward. "It's a miracle," she said, jumping into the arms of her husband, Pedro Salas. "It's happened, it really happened, I can't believe it really happened," before breaking into tears and burying her face in Pedro's shoulder.[132]

After a while I could hear that things were settling down outside, and I realized it was time for me to go, but I did so reluctantly. I was afraid I might not maintain my precious dignity once I got outside, so I decided to leave through the courtroom. I could hear the reporters peppering Kevin with questions right outside the judge's door, so I thought I might be able to sneak out the back and mingle with the crowd unnoticed. My plan was working perfectly until Len saw me and announced my arrival to a smattering of applause.

Fortunately, the reporters remained focused on Kevin. I moved to a position where he could see me and taunted him for being interviewed. Throughout the hearing we had made a game of who would defer to whom when it came to the press, and now I was sure I had won the game. Kevin knew he had lost, but he didn't care. Still trapped by the crowd in the doorway, Kevin was clearly enjoying himself.

When at last all the questions had been answered and the press went their way, it was time to go get Tony. Since there had been no actual court appearance, Tony had not been transported over. He was still many miles away, locked up in the Santa Barbara County Jail.

When we arrived at the jail, we could see where the press had gone. They were camped out on the lawn in front, waiting for what was sure to be a dramatic moment.

The grounds surrounding the jail building were on a small hill elevated just enough to see the Pacific Ocean to the West and the mountains to the East. It was just another beautiful day in Santa Barbara, made all the more enjoyable by recent events. After we had been there for some time, Len went in and met with the commander of the jail. Len knew the man, having worked with him in the past. Returning from the meeting, Len let us know it might be awhile. It seemed they felt it necessary to get the approval of the Department of Corrections.

Then, we received notice that Hilary was opposing the release. He was claiming Tony had to be returned to prison before he could be let out. Kevin began turning red as his anger burned. He immediately went into the jail and demanded to see the watch commander, with me following a safe distance behind. Soon we were in the commander's office, and Kevin wasted no time making his point. He had a valid court order demanding the immediate release of Tony Estrada, and if it were not soon honored, he would prepare the necessary contempt citation against whoever was failing to abide by it.

I noticed the red flush the watch commander's face as I attempted to put a more diplomatic spin on our request. I tried to say that we were not going to hold him personally responsible, but Kevin would have none of it. He wanted Tony out immediately, or someone in charge was going to pay for it.

When we returned outside, I told Len of our little encounter with his former colleague. Shortly thereafter, Len went in again and came back, having been told that Hilary had reversed his position and was now working with the Department of Corrections to ensure Tony's release. Len also mentioned the watch commander told him that "the little guy is not allowed in the building again."

Finally, the moment arrived. We were directed to an entrance with a small reception area, behind which was a thick steel and glass door with an electronically controlled lock. I stood toward the back as the cameramen, reporters and Tony's family and friends crowded around the outside door. We waited for what seemed like a very long time until Tony appeared behind the thick glass of the final door of his incarceration. He was wearing street clothes, the same dark slacks and long-sleeved, tan-colored shirt that he had worn five years prior on the last day of his trial. In his right hand, he carried a small plastic bag containing all of his worldly possessions, and on his face he wore a timid smile.

At last, a deputy sheriff held open the final door of Tony's imprisonment. As he walked through, a loud cheer arose from the assembled crowd. Tony barely got outside the building before the crowd pressed in around him.

I watched as Angela jumped up in the air twice, clapping her hands as she did, and then, running forward, she met him. Throwing her arms around her son for the first time in five years, she desperately held him. Embracing his mother, Tony was overcome with emotion. He couldn't speak as the tears rolled down his cheeks.

With the reporters and cameramen pressing in to capture the moment, Tony wisely asked for a chance to compose himself. Turning away and taking off his glasses to wipe away the tears, he slowly turned back to face us all, and then in a slow and soft voice he gave thanks:

> "I want to thank God, my Lord and Savior Jesus Christ
> for blessing me with this freedom.

I want to thank Judge Ochoa for his ruling, for being an honest and fair judge. I want to thank Mr. Haney, Mr. McMaster, and the rest of Ventura County that worked very hard to help this thing get through.

I want to thank my attorneys, Philip Dunn, Mr. Denoce, Investigator Len Newcomb. These guys did an excellent job of defending me.

I thank my family and friends and everybody that believed in my innocence from the beginning.

God bless you all."[133]

Of all the statements made in Tony's incredible odyssey, I thought that these carefully chosen and quietly spoken words were the most eloquent. He voiced no anger, no resentment, no self-serving remarks about his vindication—only a humble expression of appreciation to the God that made it possible and the people who believed in him.

Tony was free—free to hope, to live and to love. As he walked slowly to Len's car, I noticed that his strides were still carefully measured. It would take a while for his mind to be as free as his body, but now that day would surely come.

EPILOGUE

J UDGE OCHOA'S DECISION and order of October 24, 2001 unfortunately was not the final say in the matter. Since it was such an extraordinary ruling, there was little precedent to guide its application. For one, it was not clear whether his decision prevented the prosecution from refiling the charges and trying Tony again. Judge Ochoa later let his feelings on the issue be known by filing a subsequent order prohibiting the prosecution from re-prosecuting Tony Estrada as the Lot 10 shooter.[134]

In response, District Attorney Tom Sneddon had Jerry Franklin file a Notice of Appeal with the local District Court of Appeals.[135] While the matter remained on appeal, Tony could not be retried. But if they were successful on appeal, then they could prosecute him again on the same charges. Since it was apparent that our adversaries were not going to let it go, we responded in kind. Kevin took on Jerry by filing our response to their appeal, but more significantly Dick Hamlish filed a civil rights lawsuit in Los Angeles Federal District Court. It alleged that District Attorney Thomas Sneddon, his office, several of his deputies, and investigators, along with the City of Santa Barbara Police Department and several of its officers, violated Tony Estrada's civil rights by withholding evidence of his innocence, presenting false evidence, conspiring to obstruct justice, falsifying polygraph results, presenting false expert testimony, abusing their positions under color of authority, and knowingly and willfully allowing Tony Estrada to be falsely imprisoned.[136]

A motion to dismiss the complaint was made by all defendants based primarily on the proposition that as law enforcement officials, they were legally immune from civil liability. In the case of the prosecutors, a defense of absolute immunity was asserted for any wrong, intentional or otherwise, performed while they were acting within the scope of their employment as prosecutors. In support of their motion, two of Tony's attorneys, Duval and Chaitin, cooperated with the police department and the district attorney's office by providing them with declarations to be used as evidence. What possible motive they had for providing testimony against their former client has been the subject of much speculation.

Eventually, Judge Florence Cooper heard the motion and issued an order dismissing the entire matter.[137]

On January 2, 2003, the State Court of Appeals issued a decision reversing Judge Ochoa's ruling that Tony could not be retried as the shooter.[138] Despite the ruling, District Attorney Tom Sneddon made no effort to reopen the Lot 10 case, though he continued to state publicly that he believes Tony to be guilty of murder and that he had no regrets about how his office handled the matter.

Not long after Tony's release, Kevin threw a victory party at his house, complete with Mariachi band. It was a true cultural experience in which friends and family from the Colonia partied with Oxnard police officers, Ventura district attorneys, newspaper reporters and other assorted lawyers and investigators and their spouses. Late in the evening, after most of us were well on our way, Tony came to me with a question. Still addressing me as "Mr. Dunn," he asked, "Do you think it would be alright if I had one of those margaritas, Mr. Dunn, or do you think with everything the Lord has done for me, I shouldn't?" I expressed the opinion that the Lord made allowances for occasions such as this and reminded him of my favorite miracle, the changing of "water into wine." So Tony had his first drink since Pelican Bay.

The lawsuit of <u>Chaitin v. Dunn</u> made its way a short distance through the civil process. After our victory in the Estrada case, I made Chaitin an offer to settle for five dollars. He accepted my offer, but then refused to file a satisfaction of judgment. I made a motion to compel the filing of the document and asked for fifteen hundred dollars in sanctions against Chaitin personally. My motion was granted, and Judge Steven Hintz awarded the money. When serving the Order for Sanctions on Chaitin, I offered to satisfy the award by having him pay back the five dollars I paid in settlement. Chaitin gave me my five dollars back by way of a personal check, which I have never cashed, preferring to hold onto the check as a memento.[139]

Dennis McMaster took an early retirement from the Oxnard Police Department. The neck injury that caused him so much pain when he testified for Tony never got better. Dennis rode into the sunset like a cowboy, moving to another state and never returning. The gang unit at Oxnard P.D. never recovered. Though Dennis did everything he could to pass on his infinite knowledge of the Colonia Chiques, his instincts and personal relationships were irreplaceable. Dennis' dream of shutting down the Colonia street gang remains as distant as ever, as the Chiques are still the most feared criminal enterprise in Ventura County.

Bill Haney continued to sparkle as a Ventura prosecutor, becoming supervisor of the felony unit of the office. In my opinion, Bill was never completely comfortable as a prosecutor, having a strong, independent streak and a little too much compassion. Eventually, he decided to leave the office and go into private practice. He became a partner at the law firm of Dunn and Haney.

Kevin's star continued to shine as his private practice grew. Today he sits on the bench of the Superior Court of Ventura County, having been appointed a judge by Governor Arnold Schwarzenegger.

Having been D.A. for over twenty years, Tom Sneddon announced he would not seek another term. Not long after that, he initiated his ignominious prosecution of Michael Jackson, which he personally tried.

After their release, both Tony and Chucky moved out of Oxnard for obvious reasons. Tony went back to school, got a good job and is truly prospering. Chucky has also done well, having acquired gainful employment and successfully completing his parole period. The threat of retribution remains, however, despite the fact that Capper is still in prison. Not long after Chucky's release, I was informed that a new threat against Chucky had been issued. Less than a month later,

Chucky's sister was found dead of a heroin overdose. Not long after that, three homeboys from Colonia with EME connections paid a visit to Chucky's residence. Fortunately, Chucky wasn't home, but the homeboys made it clear they would be back. Chucky has since relocated.

Capper had some trouble adjusting to prison life. Seems he got into a fight and wound up assaulting another inmate. The local prosecutor's office filed charges and added some time to his sentence. Capper was then transferred to Pelican Bay. Upon his release, he started right up again. He wasn't out long before new drug charges and an indictment for conspiracy to commit murder sent him back to prison. As of this writing Capper has pending charges, so it is unknown just how lengthy his sentence will ultimately be.

What of Hilary and me? Well, we continued on along similar paths. A while back I agreed to take an attempted murder case against him. I couldn't resist, though it defied all common sense. The jury ultimately acquitted my client of attempted murder, thus saving him from a life sentence, and they hung up on a lesser charge.[140]

My favorite memory of Hilary will always be a chance meeting we had at U.C.L.A. It seems that not only were our kids going to the same school, but they had enrolled in the same department. When arriving in the parking lot for freshman parent orientation, I had barely set foot out of my car when I heard a familiar booming voice behind me, "Philip Remington Dunn!" The sound of his voice sent an adrenaline rush through my veins. My first reaction was he must be following me, but then I concluded it could only be a coincidence, his arriving at the very same moment.

After appropriate and polite introductions among our various family members, we spent most of the day trying to avoid one another in the seminars we were to attend. Despite our best efforts, we kept being grouped together—probably a "D" thing. Finally, I had had enough, so I decided to skip the next session and walk across campus to a safer place. I didn't get far before I turned a corner, and there in front of me was Hilary sitting on a bench. He laughed, and so did I. This was the Hilary that I liked; he met the most awkward of situations with courage and a smile.

We were forced to speak to one another about anything but the Estrada case. Turns out we had much in common. Not only were our kids going to the same university, but we had graduated from the same law school. The University of Pacific, McGeorge School of Law was a particularly brutal experience in our era, and we had the scars to prove it.

After returning to neutral corners, we shared one final moment of understanding. At the last seminar in a large amphitheater, we both could see each other across the room as various academics lectured us on the superiority of their program. Finally, as one young and particularly pompous professor began his presentation, he mentioned that he had just recently acquired his doctorate after having practiced law for five years at a prestigious law firm. He had decided that he didn't like being a lawyer; it was "too contentious." Hilary and I caught each other's eyes across the room and laughed at the same moment. We both knew what the other was thinking.

Hilary's star continued to rise in the Santa Barbara D.A.'s office. He was promoted twice, first to chief deputy and then to assistant district attorney before retiring in December 2014. I heard a rumor from colleagues in Santa Barbara that it was commonly believed that "Tom Sneddon had hung Hilary out to dry in the Estrada case and left him twisting in the breeze." It didn't change anything, but I choose to believe it just the same.

Tony and Chucky remain the closest of friends, talking to each other almost daily. Tony eventually got his college degree, taught for a while and then opened up his own business. Today he is married, with three beautiful daughters and a home of his own. He also employs between seven to ten people and brings home a six-figure income.

It is hard to say too much more about Chucky without putting him in danger. Let's just say, all things considered, he thrives. Married with children, he too has a six-figure income. A natural leader, he found a profession that could use his skills. No longer "some damn puppet on a string," he is finally his own man—as good a man as I have ever had the pleasure to have known.

About The Author

P HIL DUNN has been a celebrated trial lawyer for more than 30 years in Southern California, where he has defended people struggling in onerous situations.

For his work on People vs. Tony Estrada*, in which he proved the innocence of his client – thus overturning a murder conviction and life sentence, he received a "Local Heroes" award from the Santa Barbara Independent, and "Special Recognition" from the California State Assembly and the United States Congress from Assemblywoman Hannah Beth Jackson and Congresswoman Lois Capps.

In 2014, Phil worked to free Sgt. Andrew Tahmooressi, a former Marine diagnosed with PTSD, who was arrested at the Mexican border after making a wrong turn. Tahmooressi, in the process of moving to California to seek treatment for his PTSD, had all of his worldly possessions in his vehicle– including his legally purchased firearms, which were illegal to possess in Mexico.

As Tahmooressi's attorney, Phil was instrumental in the formation of the Mexican defense team and represented Andrew before the Consulate General's office in Baja, California. In October 2014, a Mexican District Court judge dismissed the charges on humanitarian grounds, in part due to the evidence presented that Andrew suffered from PTSD.

Crucial to Phil's familiarity with Mexican process and procedure is his humanitarian work in Mexico. Phil is a founding member of the Baja Christian Ministries (BCM), where he has helped build more

---

* Name changed to protect anonymity

than 2,000 homes for the poor, over 50 churches, and even a chapel inside Ensenada State Prison.

A prolific writer and recognized speaker, Phil regularly addresses conferences and other audiences on topics ranging from victims rights, prisoner rehabilitation and reentry, and treatment of veterans suffering from PTSD.

Endnotes

Chapter One

[1] Forensic Report of Steven McDowell, Los Angeles County Coroner's Office.

Chapter Two

[2] The Wrong Man? Santa Barbara Independent, August 23, 2001, Olivia Kinzel Reporting.

[3] Santa Barbara News Press, Slater Agrees to Bow Out of Murder Trial, October 23, 1997.

[4] People's Exhibit 24, People v. Tony Estrada, Santa Barbara Superior Court Case Number 217899.

[5] Search and Arrest Warrants signed by Judge Lodge of Santa Barbara Superior Court on January 23, 1997 for residences and persons of Gilberto Zapata, Dino Ramirez, Alfonso Rodriguez, Alfonso Martinez and Tony Estrada.

[6] Miranda v. Arizona (1960) 384 U.S. 436

[7] California Jury Instruction (CALJIC) 2.03 Consciousness of Guilt.

[8] Report of Officer Jill Johnson, City of Santa Barbara Police Department, January 26, 1997.

Chapter Three

[9] Report of Officer Mike McGrew, City of Santa Barbara Police Department, January 29, 1997.

[10] California Penal Code section 825.

[11] Gideon v. Wainwright (1963) 372 U.S. 335, established an indigent criminal defendant's right to appointed counsel at government expense.

[12] Preliminary Hearing Transcript (P.T.) of <u>People v. Tony Estrada, Dino Ramirez, Alfonso Rodriguez and Alfonso Martinez,</u> February 19, 1997 through March 11, 1997, Judge Lodge presiding, at page 1321.

[13] P.T., ibid, at p.1322.

[14] P.T., ibid, at pages 1302-1309.

[15] P.T., ibid, at page 1302.

[16] P.T., ibid, at pages 1302-1305.

[17] P.T., ibid, at p. 1323.

Chapter Four

[18] <u>California Code of Civil Procedure</u> section 170.6.

[19] <u>Brady v. Maryland</u> (1963) 373 U.S. 83.

[20] <u>California Penal Code</u> section 187.

[21] Reporter's Transcript on Appeal (R. T.), <u>People v. Tony Estrada</u>, pages 1419-1422, witness Dino Ramirez.

[22] R.T., ibid., at pages 244-269.

[23] R.T., ibid., at page 1959.

[24] R.T., ibid., at pages 1954-2076.

[25] R.T., ibid., at pages 307-383.

[26] R.T., ibid., at pages 2108-2232.

[27] R.T., ibid., at 2232-2299.

[28] R.T., ibid., pages 2319-2493, at page 2362-2363.

[29] R.T., ibid., at pages 2400-2401.

[30] R.T., ibid., at pages 2479-2480.

[31] R.T., ibid., pages 2610-2672, People's closing argument.

[32] R.T., ibid., pages 2672-2716, Defense's closing argument.

[33] R.T., ibid., pages 2733-2734.

[34] R.T., ibid., page 2778.

[35] R.T., ibid., at page 2791-2796.

[36] R.T., ibid., at page 2809.

[37] R.T., ibid., at pages 2830-2831.

[38] R.T., ibid., at page 2843.

Chapter Five

[39] California Lawyer, <u>Prison Union Muscle</u>, November, 2002, pages 24-29.

[40] San Francisco, Chronicle, <u>Guards Kill Prisoners at Pelican Bay</u>, February 24, 2000.

[41] Los Angeles Times Magazine, <u>A Necessary Evil</u>?, October 19, 2003.

[42] <u>National Youth Gang Survey of Law Enforcement Agencies</u>, 2002, U.S. Department of Justice, National Youth Gang Center of the Office of Juvenile Justice and Delinquency Prevention.

[43] MSNBC Lock Up, <u>Inside Pelican Bay 2001</u>, Forest Sawyer.

[44] 18 USC Section 1961-1968 Racketeer Influence and Corrupt Organization.

[45] San Francisco Chronicle, <u>Guards Kill Prisoners at Pelican Bay</u>, February 24, 2000.

46 San Francisco Chronicle, <u>Guards Kill Prisoners at Pelican Bay</u>, February 24, 2000.
47 California Lawyer, <u>Prison Union Muscle</u>, November, 2002.
48 MSNBC, <u>Lock Up</u>, ibid.
49 MSNBC, <u>Lock Up</u>, ibid.

Chapter Six

50 As explained to the author by Dino Duarte, Special Investigator and prison gang specialist, California Department of Corrections.
51 <u>People v. Tony Estrada</u> (1998) Second District Case Number 980A0719.
52 The actual receipt is in the possession of the author.

Chapter Eight

53 Known by the acronym <u>SODDID</u>, or <u>SODD defense</u>, sometimes used derisively by prosecutors in closing argument.
54 John 15:13, <u>The Bible</u>, New International Version, Copyright 1985, Zondervan Publishers.
55 Actually for every seven men paroled, Pelican Bay was receiving thirteen new prisoners in the year 2000. MSNBC, <u>Lock Up</u>, ibid.

Chapter Nine

56 Portions taken from <u>EDD Shootings Ventura County Ten Years Later</u>, Star Free Press, November 30, 2003.
57 R.T., ibid., at page 259, Testimony of Steven Dowell.
58 Reporter Hearing (Habeas Corpus) Transcript, (R.H.T.) Testimony of Dennis McMaster, June 5, 6 and 11, 2001.

Chapter Ten

59 R.H.T., ibid., at page 74, Testimony of William Haney.
60 <u>People v. Garcia</u> (1993) 17 Cal.App.4th 1169 Free Standing Brady Obligation.
61 "Paperwork" as defined by Detective McMaster, R.H.T., ibid., Testimony of Dennis McMaster, June 5, 6, and 11, 2001.

Chapter Eleven

62 Petitioner's Exhibit "E"; <u>"Letter by D.T."</u>, <u>In re Tony Estrada</u>; Writ of Habeas Corpus Hearing (hereafter "Writ Hearing"), Santa Barbara Superior Court Case Number 1019120.
63 Petitioner's Exhibit "B" and "C," "CD 1 and 2, C.I." <u>Writ Hearing</u>, ibid.

Chapter Thirteen

64   <u>Rules of Professional Conduct of the California State Bar, Sections 3 -700 and 4-100</u> have been interpreted as requiring a minimum of five years in certain civil matters, with seven years being a general rule of thumb. In serious felony cases that amount to "Strike Priors" the file may have to be kept for life since there is no wash out provision under the <u>California Three Strikes Law</u>. <u>Los Angeles County Bar Association Opinion No. 420 (1983).</u>

65   Matthew 10:36, <u>The Bible</u>, New International Version, Copyright 1985, Zondervan Publishers.

Chapter Fourteen

66   <u>Blacks Law Dictionary</u>, Fifth Addition, copyright 1979, p.638.

67   <u>In re Tony Estrada</u>, Order for Hearing on Writ of Habeas Corpus, dated March 2, 2001, case number 101920.

68   <u>Writ Hearing</u>, ibid., Petitioner's Exhibit "K," Transcript of Interview of Alfonso Rodriguez 5-27-01 [sic.]

69   <u>Hilary Dozer Memo to Sergeant Knapp</u> regarding March 23, 2001 meeting.

70   <u>Trial Techniques, Fundamentals of</u>, Thomas A. Mauet, page 378, Little Brown and Company, 1980 edition.

71   <u>Writ Hearing</u>, Petitioner's Exhibit "K," Transcript of Knapp and Rose, interview with Alfonso Rodriguez.

Chapter Fifteen

72   <u>Chaitin v. Dunn & Newcomb</u>, Ventura County Superior Court Case No. CIV 206274.

Chapter Sixteen

73   R.H.T., ibid., June 4, 2001, pages 1-52.

74   R.H.T., ibid., June 4, 2001, page 13.

75   Commonly known as "Use immunity," meaning the immunity only applies to testimony given at the current proceedings, <u>California Penal Code</u>, section 1324.

76   R.H.T., ibid., June 4, 2001, pages 1-73.

77   R.H.T., ibid., June 4-5, 2001, pages 1-89.

78   R.H.T., ibid., June 4-5, 2001, page 9.

79   R.H.T., ibid., June 4-5, 2001, page 54-55 and 58-60.

80   <u>California Evidence Code</u> section 915, and <u>California Code of Civil Procedure</u> section 2018.

81   R.H.T., ibid., June 5, 6 and 11, 2001, Testimony of Dennis McMaster.

82   <u>Santa Barbara District Attorney's Office Bureau of Investigation</u>, Report by Investigator Ed Shehan, February 28, 2001, "cold" interview of Detective Joe Chase.

83   <u>California Evidence Code</u> section 1230.

84   Subsequently, Capper was held in contempt and sentenced to credit for time served on June 12, 2001.

85   R.H.T., ibid., June 12-13, Testimony of "Jorge Alvarado," pages 1-314.

86   R.H.T., ibid., "Jorge Alvarado" Testimony, pages 49-50.

87   R.H.T., ibid., "Jorge Alvarado" Testimony, pages 65-66.

88   R.H.T., ibid., "Jorge Alvarado" Testimony, pages 303-304.

89   R.H.T., ibid., "Jorge Alvarado" Testimony, pages 258-260.

90   R.H.T., ibid., "Jorge Alvarado" Testimony, page 210.

91   R.H.T., ibid., "Jorge Alvarado" Testimony, pages 214-215.

92   R.H.T., ibid., "Jorge Alvarado" Testimony, page 215.

93   R.H.T., ibid., "Jorge Alvarado" Testimony, pages 292-293.

Chapter Seventeen

94   The Wrong Man?, Santa Barbara Independent, August 23, 2001, Olivia Kienzel reporting.

95   R.H.T., ibid., June 14, 2001, Testimony of William Haney, pages 1-116.

96   R.H.T., ibid., William Haney Testimony, page 21.

97   R.H.T., ibid., William Haney Testimony, pages 22-23.

98   R.H.T., ibid., William Haney Testimony, pages 26-27.

99   R.H.T., ibid., William Haney Testimony, pages 27-28.

100 R.H.T., ibid., William Haney Testimony, pages 59-61.

Chapter Eighteen

101 Writ Hearing, Petitioner's Exhibit "K" Transcript of interview Alfonso Rodriguez, 5-27-01 [sic.].

102 R.H.T., ibid., Donald Knapp Testimony, June 15, 2001 and July 3, 2001.

103 R.H.T., ibid., Donald Knapp Testimony, June 15, 2001, page 5.

104 R.H.T., ibid., Donald Knapp Testimony, June 15, 2001, page 14.

105 R.H.T., ibid., Donald Knapp Testimony, June 15, 2001, page 17.

106 R.H.T., ibid., Donald Knapp Testimony, June 15, 2001, page 20.

107 R.H.T., ibid., Donald Knapp Testimony, June 15, 2001, page 27.

108 R.H.T., ibid., Donald Knapp Testimony, June 15, 2001, page 61.

109 R.H.T., ibid., Donald Knapp Testimony, June 15, 2001, page 53.

110 R.H.T., ibid., Donald Knapp Testimony, June 15, 2001, page 76.

Chapter Nineteen

111 Writ Hearing, Petitioner's Exhibit "V," Sergeant Martel's notes.

112 Writ Hearing, Petitioner's Exhibit "S," Officer Fryslie's notes.

113 Santa Barbara City Police Report, January 26, 1997, Detective K. Aceves' interview of Juanita Zapata.

114 R.H.T., ibid., Fryslie Testimony.

115 R.H.T., ibid., Aceves Testimony.

116 R.H.T., ibid., Martel Testimony.

Chapter Twenty

[117] In re Head (1988) 43 Cal.3d 223.

Chapter Twenty One

[118] Writ Hearing, Respondent's Exhibit "14," Physical Evidence, Examination Report.
[119] Writ Hearing, Respondent's Exhibit "15," Forensic Alcohol Analysis.
[120] Defense claims blood tests clear Estrada. Santa Barbara New-Press, July 25, 2001. "We have objective scientific evidence that corroborates Mr. Estrada's testimony and impeaches the prosecution theory," quoting the author.
[121] R.H.T., ibid., August 20, 2001, closing argument of Kevin Denoce, Esq.
[122] R.H.T., ibid., August 20, 2001, closing argument of Hilary Dozer, Esq.
[123] R.H.T., ibid., August 20, 2001, page 18.
[124] R.H.T., ibid., August 20, 2001, page 15.
[125] R.H.T., ibid., August 20, 2001, pages 1-29, closing argument of Philip Dunn, Esq.
[126] R.H.T., ibid., August 21, 2001, page 23.
[127] R.H.T., ibid., August 21, 2001, page 27.

Chapter Twenty Two

[128] Decision And Order After Hearing, filed October 24, 2001, Case number 1019120.
[129] Decision And Order After Hearing, ibid., pages 63-64.
[130] Decision And Order After Hearing, ibid., page 64.
[131] Decision And Order After Hearing, ibid., page 63.
[132] KEYT NEWS, October 24, 2001.
[133] KEYT NEWS, October 24, 2001.
[134] Order After Hearing, In the Matter of Tony Estrada, On Habeas Corpus, Case Number 1019120, filed October 24, 2001.
[135] Notice of Appeal, Case No. 1019120, filed October 29, 2001.
[136] Tony Estrada v. Court of Santa Barbara, USDC, Central District of California, Case No. CV0-1-10444 FMC (AJWx).
[137] Order for Jury Trial, filed April 26, 2004.
[138] In re Tony Estrada (2003) 104 Cal.App.4th 1339.
[139] Notice of Ruling, filed September 26, 2002, Chaitin v. Dunn, et al.
[140] People v. Abel Zavala, Case No. 1075820. Verdict not guilty attempted murder, hung jury on count two, assault with a firearm, mistrial declared as to count two on September 30, 2004.